The Little Big Voice

Voice coaching for ordinary people

The Little Big Voice

Voice coaching for ordinary people

Simon Raybould

First edition 2002

08 07 06 05 04 03 02 7 6 5 4 3 2 1

ISBN 1–903689–15–5

Published by Piquant
PO Box 83, Carlisle, CA3 9GR, United Kingdom
E-mail: info@piquant.net
Website: www.piquant.net

Cover design: Jonathan Kearney
Cartoons: Andrew Stevenson

Dedication

This is for my Dad, who showed me, and all of us, that you don't need a voice at all, so long as you've got something worthwhile to say.

Contents

Acknowledgements

It's somehow weird to put just one name on the front of a book, when any book is something of a team effort. Still, as it's my name, I'd like to thank the rest of the team . . .

The first thanks *have* to be to those people who've helped me develop the ideas and methods that I've used in this book. This book is for people like you and, in a way, was written by people like you, who helped me find out what worked, what didn't, what they liked and what they didn't. They laid the whole basis for what I am trying to do here.

Elria and Piet at Piquant deserve a big thanks for taking the manuscript on, and turning it into a book; it's a real pleasure to work with you both (even if you can't skate). Andrew's cartoons are a joy to see and add an extra dimension to my text, which is very welcome. They made me giggle out loud when I first saw them, and I hope you, too, will find them a breath of fresh air.

Thanks also to Tracy for posing for the pictures, to Professors Mike Coombes and Andy Gillespie at the University of Newcastle upon Tyne for giving me time off to stick my neck out, and to Christine Henshall for taking the first interest in my idea of writing a book. Thanks are also due to Janet Longman who transcribed the words of Tué Tué from the Twi language, which is spoken in Ghana.

Last but obviously not least, *huge* thanks must also go to Isobel, my editor. What she gave back to me was clearly better than what I passed to her and I can only hope she's enjoyed it as much as I have.

So much for the 'technical' thanks. Other people deserve credit too.

First and foremost, I owe a big thank-you to Corinne (my wife, critic, proof-reader, critic, tester, critic, thesaurus, critic, fan, critic, social secretary, critic and bodyguard). She is surely the best partner a man could have. Without her very little would have happened about this book – and to be honest, very little would *ever* happen.

My children, Stephanie and Megan, are the best in the world. I suspect (well, actually I know!) that I've been too often at a computer instead of playing, but even so they offered to buy copies of this book from their pocket money, just in case no one else did. So I'm guaranteed at least two sales!

Alison, an honorary member of the family, deserves thanks for serving as my voice on many occasions for too many years.

Gerry, Clare, Eddie, Paul, Anita, Michael, Nick, Ross and numerous other friends managed to keep a straight face when I told them I was trying to write this, which gave me the confidence to carry on. My thanks to you all.

Simon Raybould
Newcastle upon Tyne

1 Setting the Scene

Philosophy and introduction – who is this book really for and what's it about? (Or 'my excuses!')

This book *isn't* for the hard-core, dedicated, been-training-for-years, my-future-is-on the-stage die-hards. It's a book for everyday people doing everyday things: people who just want to let out their voice, or who want to improve it. And that can be for personal reasons or for professional reasons. Do you want me to be more specific about who would benefit from reading it? Perhaps a list would help. (You'll find as this book goes on that I'm big on lists!)

Amateur actors and singers

Youth group leaders

Teachers

Priests and other preachers

Inhibited or nervous folk

Sports coaches

Dance instructors

Salespeople

Police officers

Counsellors

Nurses

Lecturers

Business executives

People who often get sore throats

People whose voice sometimes fails them unexpectedly

People who often go to loud parties

If you look at this list and think 'Ah yes, that's me', then I hope you find this book useful. If you aren't on the list, but find the book useful anyway, tell me! (If this ever gets as far as a second edition I can always add your category to the list, provided it's not too outrageous.)

Even if you are not on the list, remember that this small book is also for people who want a big voice just because they want a big voice. No ulterior motive – they just feel that there's something 'bigger and better' inside, but they don't know how to let it out.

The fact that you have picked up this book means that you probably fall into one of these groups. So can I ask that you stop reading this in the bookshop and take it to the till, so you can pay for it and take it home. That way you can do the exercises without embarrassing yourself, and you'll help me pay my mortgage. Everybody wins, nobody loses!

Well . . . that's the theory at least.

A quick word to dampen your spirits though, before you go any further: don't expect miracles from this book – for example, it's unlikely that working through it will get you a pay rise! (Well, I didn't get one for writing it!) However, one thing I can (almost) guarantee is that by the time you've got through this book, you should – at the very least – have developed enough of an understanding of your voice and how it works to make it far, far less likely that you'll pick up any of the voice problems listed on page 3.

The basic reason for stressing that this book is for 'normal' people is this: it's my belief that everyone has an interesting voice.

Everyone's *voice* is interesting, simply because every*body* is interesting. Even *bores* are interesting! That's because you can spend time thinking about how they got to be that way. And because your voice – its style and its volume – stems from the whole of your body, what you *are* is reflected in what you *sound like*. Think about it . . . bores have boring *voices*, don't they?

That's a key point, and I'll keep coming back to it in the pages ahead so often you'll get bored of it. You see, once you understand that your voice is a product of your whole body, lots of ideas follow. Not only does it mean that everyone's voice is *interesting*, it also means that everyone's voice is *different*. Your voice is as unique as your fingerprints and retinal patterns.

And just as complicated.

It also means that there's no such thing as a bad voice (you can have bad ways of *using* your voice and *bad habits* with your voice – and I don't just mean talking loudly during a romantic scene in a film – but your voice *itself* isn't bad). So if you are at the point of saying 'I just can't do that: my voice is rubbish', think again. It can't be true that your voice is rubbish without your whole body – from your feet all the way up to your scalp – being tarred with the same brush, and that simply can't be the case.

All this may sound like metaphysical psychobabble for now, so perhaps you should just take my word for it at the moment. You'll get a better idea about what I mean by the end of the book – assuming you get that far!

Silence is golden – but only when you've chosen not to speak!

Time for a quick word of warning; I'm sorry it has to be so early in the book!

Almost no one is immune from the risk of damaging their voice. If you find yourself speaking lots, or loudly (or worse, both!) then there's a chance you might end up overdoing things. This isn't an exhaustive list, but you might want to take particular care if –

- you sometimes have a sore throat by the end of the working day
- you get a sore throat more often than the rest of your family
- your voice sometimes fails you and doesn't come out as you expect[1]
- you lose your voice
- there is pain of any kind when you use your voice
- people have to listen hard to hear what you're saying.

I've even heard of people needing treatment for their voice because they were 'trying too hard' when they used their computer's speech recognition software! Obviously there's more to using your voice than meets the eye (well, the ear, but you know what I mean!).

The kinds of damage you can do when you abuse your voice include things like vocal nodules and cysts on and around your voice box, laryngitis, and even ulcers on your vocal cords, where the membranes are worn

---

[1] This is, of course, assuming you're not an adolescent whose voice is 'breaking' – in which case, you're on your own!

away by misuse. In most cases, the symptom you notice first – assuming you're paying proper attention to your body! – is hoarseness, but sometimes these problems can ambush you, leaving you literally speechless . . .

The good news is that the damage isn't *usually* permanent, although it can be pretty long-term and debilitating. The golden rule is simple: if in doubt, do something about it. By the way, as you go through this short book, you might find yourself getting tired. Don't worry, that's normal. If you find your throat getting tired, however, stop and take a break. It's usually a sign that you're carrying tension in places where you shouldn't. I've tried to flag places where this can happen as you go through the exercises in this book. Just use some common sense and you'll be fine.

Feelings – what you hear isn't what you get

And while we're at it, here's another key point: you never know exactly what your own voice sounds like. Most of what you hear of your own voice comes to your ears along the bones in your head, but what other people hear gets to their ears by travelling through the air, so you can't assume that you always sound like you *think* you sound! So, don't just listen to yourself, see if it *feels* right.

Now that probably sounds like more psychobabble, but think of it like this: if you play tennis, when you're learning your overhand serve, you know you've got it right when it hits the sweet spot in the middle of the racket so that the ball just ziiiiings over the net. You don't need to see it or hear it, or anything else, because you can feel it the very second the ball leaves your racket. In the same way, you'll *feel* it when you're using your voice properly.

The background to most of what's in this book is theatre techniques. Why? Well it's pretty simple really, if actors from the Royal Shakespeare Company can make their voices reach the back row of huge theatres with no microphones and without shouting, then you've *no* excuse for not being able to make everyone in your school, church hall, football field, or wherever able to hear your constructive and enlightening comments.[2] What's more, you can do it without shouting, and without sounding stressed, boring or pushy!

---

[2] Such as your views on the referee's eyesight and understanding of the offside rule.

Organisation – a nice idea, shall we try it?

This book is chopped up into sections which I have called 'parts', and – within them – into 'bits'. But don't be fooled, that's just a convenient way of organising things. Your voice doesn't come in parts or bits, so don't get hung up on the fact that you are having a problem with something some-where in part two, for example. If things aren't going right for you there, don't panic! Just make sure you've understood at least enough to be able to get the general idea and move on to another part of the book. You can come back to it later. (In fact, I'll go so far as to say you *should* come back to it . . . and not too much later at that.)

If you've read something several times, and kept coming back to it, because it just doesn't make sense to you, it's probably because I've writ-ten it badly, so you should think about dropping me a line to ask for clari-fication.

That said, it's always a good idea to have a go at the exercises in each chapter before going too far on, particularly for those times when exercises build on each other.

Theory – some background for what's to follow

Don't expect some great anatomical discussion here – that's not my style or intention. Instead, what I'm going to do is give you a framework that ex-plains how the rest of this book is organised.

For simplicity's sake, lets split up how people talk into five parts:

• Power

• Generation

• Control

• Content

• Reception

The last two are pretty well outside the scope of this book: what you say and how people listen to you haven't got all that much to do with voice. There's not a lot I can do (in a book) to make *what* you say more interesting . . . and there's no power on earth that can allow you to control the reception – that is, how your audience perceives what you're saying to them – or at least not very much. (Apart from paying them vast sums of money, of course, but that's probably cheating.) So here we're going to concentrate on the first three parts. Let's start by getting a very rough idea of how these are related to different parts of your body.

Power equates to breathing, which happens in your torso (don't underestimate it – breathing is absolutely fundamental to voice). *Generating sounds* is the miraculous bit (and believe me, if you think about it, it is a miracle). It's the process of turning simple, moving air into sound or noise – it's the bit

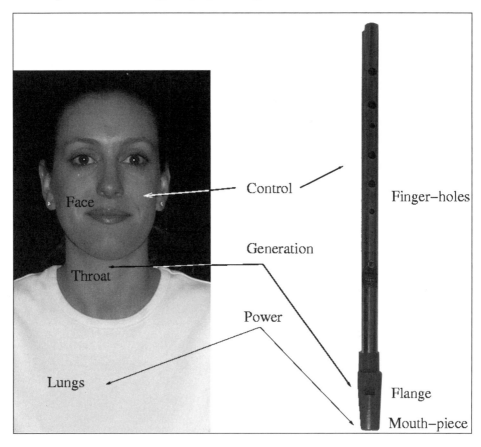

Figure 1

that happens in your throat. *Control* is the way we change simple sounds into something worth listening to – words – and that is done in your mouth. Okay, so I'm generalising, but it's a useful tool.

Have a look at Figure 1.

Comparing a person to a penny whistle might seem rather odd, but think of it like this: the mouthpiece of the whistle is where the moving air is generated (like your lungs); the little hole in the front (technically it's called a flange, by the way) is your throat – where the moving air is used to create sounds; and the various holes that are covered or left open are your mouth, with complicated combinations of shapes for your lips, tongue and so on. (Obviously, with a whistle, you have to learn the right way to produce the right sounds, just as a baby has to enthusiastically practise making sounds while it gradually learns to shape them into words [3]).

Here's a summary of this lot:

What?	How?	Where?
Power	Breath	Torso
Generation	Sound	Throat
Control	Words	Mouth area

The rest of this book is built around these three elements, although I also deal with some other odds and ends in later sections.

The nature of sound – what are we playing with anyway?

There's something we probably need to get cleared up before we go too much further, and that's the nature of 'sound' and how your voice generates it. Otherwise things are going to get pretty difficult to explain later on.

Sound is just bouncing molecules. Think of someone playing a violin by drawing the bow over the string. This makes the string vibrate so fast that it looks a bit blurred because it's shaking so fast that your eyes can't quite get a fix on it. As the string bounces from side to side, it sets air molecules bouncing into each other. These in turn crash into other air molecules – passing the *energy* of the sound along in the process – before returning to more or less where they started. The newly moving molecules repeat the process and bounce into their neighbours, and so on until the sound is carried away from the violin and towards your ear. It's interesting (but not desperately important) to remember that only the *energy* moves, and that although the air molecules wobble around bashing into each other, their *net* movement is pretty well zero. Figure 2 shows you what I mean.

---

[3] In the case of several people I can think of, this is only part of the process – if only they could now learn to *stop!*

When the vibration reaches your ear, it sets off a vibration in bones and things in your ear, which in turn set tiny hairs moving inside your ear. The movement of these hairs triggers tiny electrical pulses in the nerves to your brain. The brain then interprets these electrical signals as different sounds.

That's why you should never try *just* listening to yourself. The sounds generated by your own voice don't generally travel through the air, but instead they move more through the bones of your jaw. This gives them a

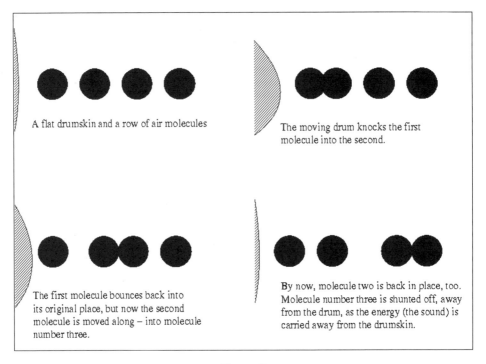

A flat drumskin and a row of air molecules

The moving drum knocks the first molecule into the second.

The first molecule bounces back into its original place, but now the second molecule is moved along – into molecule number three.

By now, molecule two is back in place, too. Molecule number three is shunted off, away from the drum, as the energy (the sound) is carried away from the drumskin.

Figure 2

different 'flavour' because bone molecules bounce differently from air molecules. For a start, they can't move around as much because they're part of a solid structure (your jaw!).

There's an obvious question about all of this. If sound is just air molecules bouncing into each other, carrying sound towards your ear from the source of the sound, what is it, exactly that happens in your throat to start those molecules vibrating when you speak? Well for a start, don't get confused by the name that people often give to the part of your throat where this all happens: the vocal cords. This gives an image of the air from your lungs blowing over thin cords stretched across your throat, which the passing air sets moving . . . a bit like using a set of bellows to set harp strings vibrating. Far too much like hard work!

For a simple understanding, go back to the idea of the penny whistle. As the air is pushed out of your lungs, it moves up through your throat at quite a speed. If your throat is totally relaxed, the air passes up and out of your mouth without anything happening at all.

What we often call the vocal cords might be better thought of as the vocal folds – essentially they're two bits of cartilage with lots of muscles attached to them. When you want to make a noise, these folds are brought close together, pretty well blocking off the airway in your throat. The air that's being pushed out of your lungs will eventually force them open (because the muscle that does this pushing – called your diaphragm – is stronger than your vocal fold muscles). When it does, the air pressure in your throat drops as the air rushes through and the vocal folds close again. The air pressure immediately below them rises again, and so the process is repeated. It's this repeated opening and closing (really, really quickly[4]) that's the basic vibration of the sound of your voice. Incidentally, when the air rushes out and the air pressure is lowered (because the air molecules between your vocal folds are moving so fast) the phenomenon is called the Venturi effect. That's the same effect that gives planes lift as the air passes over their wings. Cool, huh?

I find it often helps to imagine the process as a lot like whistling, with the vocal folds doing the same job as your lips do (even though it's not exactly what happens). Hang onto these ideas, because they will help you (I hope!) understand some of the ideas and exercises later on.

Right then . . . on to part two, all about generating *Power*.

---

[4] On average, it's about 125 times per second for a man, and around 250 for a woman – which is why women's voices tend to be higher pitched than men's.

2 Power

Exercises to start off with

Before we do anything else, let's go right in with some practical exercises. We can *talk* about things later!

First things first: lie down on your back and get comfortable. The first step to being comfortable is probably to make sure that you are lying on a carpet, or at the very least on a nice, big, snuggly towel. You may also find that you need to rest your head on something firm (a couple of paperbacks are usually a good bet), but try not to tip your head too far forward. If you do, you'll find that you've bent your windpipe forwards, which will make it a little more difficult for you to breathe out.

Check the gap between the small of your back and the floor. Everyone's different, remember, so don't take this bit too literally, but it's usually a good idea to get relatively flat to the ground. If you can only just get your fingers between your back and the floor (with a little contortion of your arm) then stay as you are. On the other hand, if you're anything like me and you can almost make a fist in the gap, then bend your legs up at the knees so that you can put your feet flat on the floor. This should help you get your back closer to the floor.

Now, put your left hand in the middle of your chest (somewhere around the midpoint of your chest bone) and your right hand over your stomach and breathe deeply. Generally, I find that people's right hands tend to end up around their belts, and their left hands somewhere around dead-centre. The photo in Figure 3 should give you a better idea of what to do.

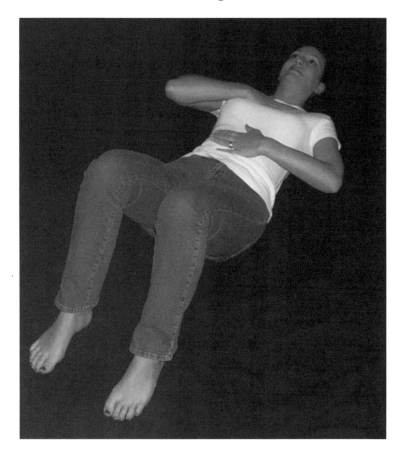

Figure 3

You should find that your hands are moved by your body as you breathe in and out. Make sure that you don't move your hands by using your arms – try and keep them totally relaxed – but concentrate on feeling your hands *being* moved as you breathe. That's your chest expanding and contracting as you breathe in and out.

Experiment to see whether you can adjust your breathing so that only one hand at a time is moved. Don't worry if you can't, as we'll come back to this in a few minutes.

Let's take a brief pause for a moment (you can sit up to read this bit!) to look at the mechanics of how your breathing works. There are actually two ways of getting air into your lungs. Both work the same way: they just increase the size of your chest so that your lungs expand, which reduces the air

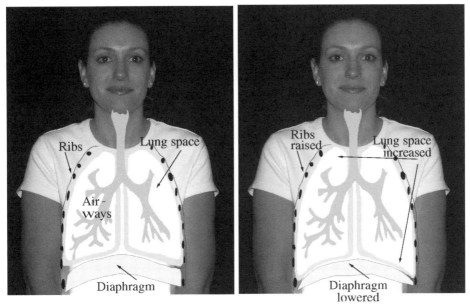

Figure 4

pressure in them and leads to air being sucked in. It's as simple as that! Nothing complicated about it. The illustration in Figure 4 shows it as a sketch.

The two ways differ only in terms of how the chest is made bigger. You can do it by pulling your ribcage up (using the external intercostal muscles, if you're interested) or by lowering your diaphragm – the big muscle between your chest and your stomach area. When you do it the first way, the muscles involved are small, although there are lots of them. This means that raising your ribcage is a poor way of going about things: you've little control over how quickly the air comes back out and these muscles can get tired pretty fast.

On the other hand, using your diaphragm gives you much more stamina and a far more subtle control over how fast the air comes out. This is a good thing! What's more, your lungs are larger at the bottom than at the top, and you can expand more down there too, meaning that you can get more air in.

Okay, back to the exercise. Get back on the floor, with one hand on your chest and the other on your diaphragm. Concentrate on getting *only* your diaphragm hand to move. I've found that most people find it's easier to do this bit with their eyes closed, and I'd very strongly recommend doing it when there's no one around, and with the phone turned off. Getting disturbed at the wrong moment can be really frustrating.

There's no magic formula for getting only your diaphragm hand to move. To be honest, it's pretty instinctive. It's the way we naturally breathe when we're very young – just look at a peacefully sleeping baby and you'll see what I mean. Come to think of it, if you listen to an uncomfortable baby, you'll get an idea of how much *power* can be generated by someone using their diaphragm to tell someone that 'I'm-hungry-what's-taking-you-so-long-I've-been-calling-for-*seconds*!'

Essentially, all this exercise is trying to do is to get you to breathe like a baby. Use your diaphragm (and a couple of other tricks you'll learn about later) to *power* your voice and you can make the same amount of noise, if that's what you want . . . and as you're bigger than a baby, you can make more noise than a baby!

Once you've got your breathing under control, take a few minutes to listen to it and to get the pattern of it fixed in your mind.[5] You'll be coming back to that pattern quite a lot, so it's worth taking a little time to get used to it.

Now, at the moment all you're doing is breathing, not making any sounds, right? (If you *are* making a sound, check that your head isn't too far forward, as any kinks you put into your windpipe can mean you get a kind of whistling effect as you exhale.) If your mouth and throat are open and straight – well, straight*ish* anyway! – you shouldn't be making much noise at all.

But all that's going to change.

Imitating a baby – making your first sounds

Now, each time you exhale, let your throat tighten a very, very little. You'll find you're making a kind of vague grunting noise. Be careful not to overwork your throat, otherwise you'll end up producing a sound like a snoring bulldog with adenoid problems! Make sure you've not changed the pattern of your breathing, and check that you're still breathing only with your diaphragm by checking your hands. If things have gone wrong, go back to the start and work yourself though the exercise from the beginning; there's no point in rushing this one.

Next, and very gradually, begin to push fractionally more air out of your lungs each time you exhale. Do it by making a slightly sharper movement with your diaphragm. This will push more air through your throat and mouth

---

[5] By this I mean the rate at which you breathe in and out.

and you'll find that the amount of noise you make increases slightly. (Remember what I said about doing this alone? Now's *not* the time to suddenly discover that your best friend has remembered she can use her key to your place any time she likes!)

There are a few things to beware of at this stage:

- Make sure that you carry on breathing from your diaphragm only – don't start moving your shoulders or the top half of your chest any more than you were doing before.

- Make sure that you're not getting dizzy or starting to hyperventilate. Because you're pushing more air into and out of your lungs than usual, there's more oxygen in your blood than you're used to. It can make you a bit light-headed. If it does, just stop for a moment to settle down, then start again; it's no big deal.

- Make sure that you keep your shoulders relaxed and that your neck stays unstressed too.

- Make very sure that you're not doing anything more with your throat than the very minimum necessary to make the Uuuhhhhh sound. The 'pipe' between your mouth and your lungs (the trachea, officially) should stay open and clear as far as possible.

- Make sure that you don't cheat, by letting the extra air out and making your Uuh sounds slightly longer. You'll come to that later, but for now, just let the extra air out in your usual amount of time and you'll get extra volume. If you check that your breathing pattern hasn't changed, you should be okay.

Don't be tempted to rush this exercise, as it's quite a lot trickier than it sounds. I've noticed people often think that turning on the CD or the radio will help them to stay relaxed and make this whole (bizarre) exercise less intimidating. Generally, I tell people to do that if they have to, but that usually it's better not to. The music often actually gets in the way. People end up listening to the music, instead of concentrating. What's even worse, the beat of the music often has an effect on how fast you breathe. From Mozart to the Manics, it's all rhythmic!

Once you've got comfortable with making your noise a bit louder, make more and more of an effort to push the volume up. Do it gradually, no faster than you're comfortable with, but it's important that by the end you should really, really be going for it, flat out. (Before you get too carried away, though, check carefully that you're not just shouting. The key thing to check is whether your throat is simply a tube, or whether it feels like it's doing any of the work.)

It's a bit like a sneeze. If you're not sure whether you've sneezed or not, you haven't! Similarly, if you're not sure that you've gone far enough and loud enough with this exercise, you haven't! (OK, that's not literally the case, so just keep an eye on yourself, but I've found far, far more people under-work at this stage than attempt to overwork. In fact, you can't really overwork this one, except when you get to the point where you're having problems with items from the list above.)

When you feel that you've finished this exercise, you can move on to the most important activity in the book, and one that we'll return to again and again . . .

. . . go make yourself a cup of tea and relax. Come back when you've had a break.

Making progress – more baby noises

Welcome back. So far, so good.

Now for the bad news: before starting any of the new exercises in this little section, you should repeat all the exercises you've just done. Go slowly. To be blunt, it's better to make no progress than to make progress too fast as you'll only come a cropper in the end. As this is the most basic bit of the whole shooting gallery, it's worth spending as much time on it as it needs.

Obviously, as you get more experienced, you'll be able to zip through this basic exercise in less and less time. Eventually it will become routine and you'll not have to think about it. Until that day, however . . . concentrate.

Once you've got back to where you finished before your tea break it's time to move on. This time, instead of trying to let out the extra air in the same amount of time (making more noise) try letting the extra air out over a few seconds more. Do it gradually, adding just half a second or so every few times you exhale. With a bit of practice, you should be able to double the time you can maintain a sound. Don't panic if you don't instantly manage that though – remember my assertion earlier in this book that your voice was organic and a part of your whole person? Well, if that's the case, it follows that different people will change at different rates. Work at the rate that's best for you.

The next obvious step is to combine the two exercises, but first . . .

. . . have another break.

A quick word about breaks, before we go any further. Little and often is best, and you should always stop an exercise before you get tired and start to go wrong. In an ideal world, you should always stop while you're doing it right. This is because getting it right is all about muscle memory. It's like learning to play a piece on the piano, or serving overhand at tennis, or anything else that you think of . . . much easier to do than to describe (but you know when you've got it right, because the ball just ziiiiings off the racquet). It's not something that you can remember 'in your head', just as you can't play a complicated piece of music by thinking about everything all the time. There's just too much to think about: your brain can't process information fast enough to give instructions to your arms, wrists and fingers about what notes to hit.

But while your brain can't do it consciously, your body can do it without all the *thinking* bits. Once you've practised a few times, you'll find that you can do the exercises without your brain getting involved much at all.

By the way, if you're doing these floor exercises – and the ones that follow – quite a lot, it's worth just reading the next couple of paragraphs. They tell you how to sit up. The way *not* to do it is by tightening your stomach muscles and doing the altogether-far-too-athletic (but impressive) sit-up, in which you pull yourself upright using only the muscles in your torso. Doing that inevitably leads to you tightening up muscles that you want to keep pretty relaxed. It also means, I've found, that you're more likely to suffer from Postural Hypotension, which is the fancy medical term for that slightly spaced-out feeling you get when you move too suddenly and feel like you've left your blood behind. (If that *does* happen, by the way, just wait it out.)

So what's the best way to sit up? Well, different folks prefer different ways, but a really good technique that I've used is to roll onto my side, then curl into a slightly foetal position, and from there use my arms to push myself more or less upright. The downside is that this technique tends to twist the spine ever so slightly, but that's generally okay at this point.

Imagining things – picturing your sound

Right, back to the exercises. You've used the basic pattern of . . .

1. Lie on your back and get your position right

2. Establish your natural breathing pattern

3. Establish where you're breathing from

4. Take control of where you're breathing from to boost the amount of work done by your diaphragm

5. Start to make slight, unfocused vocalisations

6. Make those vocalisations louder by moving your diaphragm more markedly

7. Repeat from the beginning, but this time making your vocalisations longer

. . . to get yourself started off.

Once you've started to get the hang of it, there are several add-ons you can use to make the exercises more interesting. They come in the form of simple visualisations (which is just fancy jargon for your imagining you can see something). You can make up your own, of course, if the ideas here don't work for you, but they work pretty well for me.[6]

- Imagine you're a fountain with a beach-ball balanced on the top. Your job is to keep the beach-ball up in the air for as long as possible. It shouldn't wobble about too much and it shouldn't get lower or higher either. The trick is to imagine the sound you're making as the stream of water, and keep it constant.

- Once you've really got the hang of balancing that ball, try variations, such as making your sound softer, so that the ball sinks towards your mouth, and then pushing it away again, all in the same breath.

- Find something on the ceiling that attracts your attention – preferably something that shouldn't be there. Use your body as a weapon which fires small balls of 'voice' at the offending article. (I find this exercise particularly easy in rooms with patterned ceilings or flaky paintwork.) Be careful not to get too carried away – your body should remain relaxed – and you need to make sure that you don't have to move your head out of position in order to aim your vocal bullets. (If you do, either pick another target or move your whole body around.)

- Anything else you can think of!

Don't get too hung up on the nature of these visualisations. They're a means to an end, not an end in themselves. Once you've got the hang of the basic exercise, they're just a way of getting you to do some more work without thinking about it too much. After all, the aim is to get you to the point where you don't concentrate on how you're using your voice at all, leaving you free to think about what you're saying, but with a bigger repertoire of voice to support it. If the visualisation makes you feel inhibited, then it's not working for you, and you should do something else that you find more comfortable.

---

[6]   Which probably says more about my state of mind than I care to admit, but . . . anything to make these exercises less tedious!

By now, of course, you may also want to move on from making a vague Uuh sound – after all, when you repeat it often enough, it can sound horribly like the soundtrack to a particularly silly Jim Carrey film! The next step towards actually making a useful sound is to change your Uuh to an Ah. As you do this, make sure that you keep your mouth nicely open – though not so open that it puts stress on any muscles – and that you continue to do the rest of the exercise properly. You'd be surprised at how often people need to go right back to the beginning and start again, simply because when they started to think about making a different sound, they forgot about *how* they were making the first sound. Check, and if you're not doing it as you should be, go back and run through the whole process again from the beginning.

And as you're doing it, remember the most important rule . . . if you're bored or tired, have a break!

Spectacular progress – baby's first words

Once you're back at it, you'll need to revise what you have done right back from the beginning before you can try a number of variations on the Ah theme. Try adding various plosives in front of the Ah. (A plosive is a letter like P or B, where the sound is made by holding the lips together until they are forced open in a kind of ex*PLOS*ion of sound.) You'll end up with words like baah and paah (and maybe even taah or vaah, which strictly aren't plosives at all, but will do for now).

The final stage of work on your back (as I'm sure you'll be pleased to know!) is to add second syllables to your words. You can use nonsense words if you want to, but often that means you get too hung up on the act of inventing the word – so I've saved you the trouble and done it for you. What I suggest is that you recite some (or all) of these words:

Maarley

Baarley

Taarley

Faarley

Caarley

Daarley

Chaarley

Remember to try and keep the first vowel – the long A – as the important bit of the word. Actually, don't treat them as words, just as Ah sounds with bits added. And don't forget to keep checking that the power is coming from the right place, and that you've not developed any of the bad habits I listed earlier.

Once you've got yourself comfortable with Maarley and so on, try to run two of them together without breaking for breath. Start with just two in one breath at first, then three, and so on. However, before you add the next word to your list, stretch the length of the words you're saying. In other words, you should be saying 'Maaaaaaaaaaaaaarly' before you say 'Maarely Baarley'. Moving on to an extra word should actually shorten the amount of breath you're using in terms of duration, so you can use the spare breath to increase the volume of what you say. Eventually, you'll be able to go through the full list of words in one breath (and quite loudly at that!).

By the way, did I mention the fact that you may want to do this on your own and with the door locked? (I once had a group session of this exercise interrupted by a nervous security guard who wanted to know what was going on – he'd had reports of a witch's coven meeting on the premises!)

You'll find that a lot of serious books[7] about voice make you go through dozens of exercises at this point, playing with all the possible combinations of vowels and starting consonants (Maa May Mee Mo Muu, Taa Tay Tee To Tuu, and so on) but frankly, I feel life is too short for that.[8]

The last exercise in this part of the process – which once again you should work up to from the beginning – involves real sentences, rather than the rubbish you've been speaking up until now. Because thinking of what to say tends to stress people, I'm going to give you a few nice and easy starting sentences, but if you find my prose too boring, make up your own, by all means. The one thing I *would* strongly recommend, however, is that you make up your own sentence before you start to speak. Don't try to talk and think at the same time, it's too difficult (as many politicians prove every time they do an interview):

---

[7]   There are some fantastic books out there on the market, and I list a few of them later on. If you're deadly serious about a career in acting, for example, you should consider moving on to them once you've finished here. For the more usual person-on–the-street, exercises like those tend to be counter-productive because, frankly, they're just no fun!

[8]   Don't get me wrong, I'm not saying they aren't good exercises, but if you're the kind of person that they're aimed at, then you'll probably have given up on this book and thrown it away in disgust by now in any case.

Automatic opening makes me maudlin.

Focus ought to be automatic.

Arbitration alone is always arduous.

Opening cars can't be hated.

Alive is a very obvious word.

Amateur actors always argue.

Cartons can't be calculated.

As the stress of thinking about what to say tends to make people nervous – and therefore more likely to make mistakes (and realise it!) – it's important to avoid thinking too much. On the other hand, you need to make some progress towards free speech. One trick people often find useful here is to make up a message for their answering machine (or something similar). These types of messages tend to contain things that you're very familiar with – such as your name, presumably – and are unlikely to be too long or complicated, so that you don't need to think too hard. They make a good, short exercise. (Obviously if you've got a hang-up about answering machines and they make you nervous, you should think about doing something else, but this trick seems to work for most people).

Remember – always! – while you're doing each exercise that you need to remember the basic points about where your breath should be coming from. Keep checking that you are not developing any of the bad habits I listed earlier. If you find you've got a problem, go back!

One for the album – baby's first steps

Obviously, everything we've done so far has been of very little practical value, because you've been flat on your back for most of it. You *can* try and do your talking for the rest of your life lying down, but you might not find it terribly helpful in the long run! But now is the time to try it the hard way – standing up. Don't worry if it all goes horribly wrong at this point, as it's harder to do standing up.

The things to watch out for as you try this all have to do with getting tense. Often this is caused not only by the realisation that what you are doing is actually quite tricky but also by your posture. On the floor it was (relatively) easy – gravity was on your side and you didn't need to keep your balance, but when you're standing you've got to keep everything lined up correctly too, or you'll end up putting unwanted tension into your muscles.

Fortunately, there's an easy way of finding out the 'right' position for your body to be in, and it won't take much practice at all. It's a game called Rag Dolls.

Stand with your feet comfortably apart and get yourself relaxed. Then, flop forwards like a rag doll, so that your hair falls toward the ground and your head is upside down between your knees – or lower if you can. It's *very* important *not* to keep your head raised, and you might find it easier if you bend your knees slightly. Have a look at the picture in Figure 5 for a guide to the right way of doing it. Once you've turned yourself into a rag doll, start to uncurl from your feet up. (Be careful not to lead with your head at any time, even as you get near the top. *Figure 6 shows someone making this mistake.* You'll be amazed how hard it is to leave yourself vulnerable by keeping your head down all the time.) I sometimes find it helpful to think of TV wildlife programmes showing speeded-up sequences of flowers pushing up through the soil, growing a little, then pulling their flowers around to be facing upwards to the sun. If that image is helpful, fine . . . if you've no idea what I'm talking about, just ignore it!

You'll know when to *stop* uncurling because you'll have gone through what we call the body neutral position, a moment when your head was perfectly balanced on your neck and it took almost no effort to keep it there. Stop as soon as you feel your neck muscles having to start to do some work to hold your head up again, and move ever so slightly back to the point of perfect balance. It might take a few tries to get used to finding this position, but once there you'll find it easier than ever to get your diaphragm breathing sorted out while standing up.

In fact, it's actually easier to get the diaphragm stuff to work standing up – in principle – because you've got gravity on your side. But it *feels* much more difficult because you have to remember to stand up at the same time . . . and standing up is a lot more complicated than it sounds.[9]

Sadly, I've now got to give you some very bad news. You've got to start all over again. By that I mean that you've got to go back to the basic routine before you do anything else – if necessary, go all the way back and do all the exercises on the floor first:

1. Get your position right.

2. Establish your natural breathing pattern.

---

[9]   Ask any drunk or watch any toddler!

3. Establish where you're breathing from.

4. Take control of where you're breathing from to boost the amount of work done by your diaphragm.

5. Start to make small, unfocused vocalisations.

And now, there's the added complication of doing a rag doll at the start, so that you do all of this in your body neutral position.

It may be depressing to realise that you've now got to do everything you did on the floor all over again, so I'll just take a moment here to point out a couple of things to make you feel more positive (and less likely to be rude about this book to your friends).

- Now that you know what you're looking for, namely diaphragm control, it's easier to find it, so you should make progress at least as quickly as on the floor, if not faster.

- It's not anything you have to get done all at once, so you can do it as and when you've got time – there's no rush.

- There's less preparation involved now, so you can more easily do the exercises in short spurts (while waiting for the kettle to boil, for example!).

- You won't feel so embarrassed if someone finds you because you're not lying down looking silly.

- If you get your body neutral position absolutely correct it's not too much more difficult to do than when you're lying down, so you should rattle through this bit.

Remember the visualisations I suggested earlier on? Now that you're standing up, there's a whole new world of things you can imagine. I can't stress often enough that you should make sure you've still got the basics right now that you're upright, but assuming you have, have a go at some of these:

- Find a painting or similar thing on the wall, and imagine the continuous stream of sound you're making is going to be used to outline that object. Move around the object slowly.

- Repeat that one. Next you aren't trying merely to outline the object, but to cut away the wall around it – your voice is a laser cutting a hole in the wall, so it needs to be both loud and continuous.

- Focus on a light switch, and imagine turning the lights off and on by forcing small bits of sound to hit the switch with enough force to tip it.

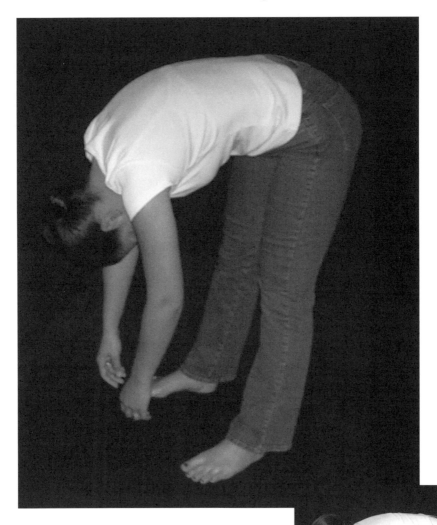

Figure 5
(inset Figure 6)

- Repeat number three using actual words instead of just short Ah sounds. Fortunately the words *on* and *off* are quite suitable vocally!

- Find a door that's ajar and imagine pushing it closed with your voice. Doors are heavy (compared to sound) so you'll have to push hard.

- Imagine the door has a spring, so that whenever you stop pushing, it starts to swing open again.

This section has been aimed at getting you raw *power* that you can use for whatever you want. If it's worked, great, if it hasn't, try looking over the next bit. Think of it as a checklist of things that might be causing you a problem. (It's quite a long list but don't be daunted. It's worth making *absolutely* sure there are no problems waiting in the wings ready to make your life more difficult later on.) Come to think of it, it wouldn't do you any harm to read it through, just to be sure, even if you're happy with what you've got.

Problems, problems, problems

I've found that most of the problems people have at this stage can be roughly grouped into a few categories:

1. Getting all tensed up. If you get too wound up, your neck will go stiff and you'll probably have your head at the wrong angle too. Make a point of dropping your shoulders . . . and then drop them again. Some people can even drop them a third time. Smile. Remember that there's no such thing as a bad voice, so you've got nothing to be worried about and nothing to prove. Relax yourself and shake out a bit, then do your rag doll again to get yourself back in position.

2. Getting scared. This sometimes makes you tense, so see the note above, but here are some other things to look out for.

   - Not vocalising all the way through your exhalation because you're nervous about the amount of noise you're making – unvoiced breath sneaks out at the start or end (or both!) of your out-breath.

   - Letting out all the air but not using some of it. This one is a bit more subtle than the last, but essentially it's the same thing. Here you'll probably find that your voice sounds a bit 'breathy' – which is pretty well exactly what it is! You're using only *some* of the air you're exhaling to make a sound, but simultaneously letting the rest out as a kind of hiss which sounds a bit like a leaky pipe.

- Strangling the sound. By this I mean that you're trapping the air that your lungs are trying to exhale by keeping your throat so tight it can't get out. Watch out for this one, as it can give you problems related to sore throats and so on – you've got energy which has to go somewhere, so it ends up in the walls of your throat.

3. Getting slap-dash or lazy. Thinking about it, this isn't too much of a surprise – particularly not if you've been bashing through this book in a relatively short period of time. Perhaps I should more generously call it 'getting tired'. When it happens (and it happens to everyone at some point) just stop. Do something else. Have a rest. Write an e-mail or a letter[10] to a friend telling them how good this book is. Make a cup of tea. Whatever.

4. Getting too excited. This is the one I enjoy most! It sometimes happens that when you're going through your exercises – everything suddenly falls into place. You 'root' the sound of your voice. The room resonates and you probably startle yourself. That's *not* a problem! You're *supposed* to sound like that: that's your *real* voice. When it happens, I find that people are often so taken aback that one or other of the 'scared' problems pops up. If it happens to you, relax and don't be tempted to keep trying and trying in an attempt to make it happen again. It's like hunting butterflies – chasing after it is pretty well a waste of time. Stop, rest, try again later. In the meantime, write a letter!

I'd like to step out of the list for a moment (yes, I know, it's a long moment) and just talk about point four. I might have given you the impression that you're at fault if that epiphany doesn't happen for you. You're not. There are other things that you may need to get sorted out before you can reasonably expect to get a rooted voice. But if you *do* happen to get lucky, celebrate! The first time I managed it, it was such a surprise to me that I got completely unnerved and couldn't manage to relax enough to achieve it again for the next two weeks . . .

I've also known people who've found their rooted voice and asked if they needed to carry on coming to a voice class (or whatever we were working in). The answer is that they don't *need* to. I'd like to think that they'd *like* to come back later, to develop some more once they'd got used to what they'd just discovered, but it might be worthwhile for them to just take a little time to enjoy the voice they've found and get used to it.

---

[10] Don't phone!

And it certainly can take some getting used to. It's rather like the experience of the brunette reporter who dyed her hair blonde, and then found that men looked at her differently (more?). It's possible that people may find 'the new you' a bit startling until they get more used to it. Your new (improved!) voice can be the vocal equivalent of newly dyed hair . . . enjoy!

Okay, now back to the list . . .

5. Trying too hard. If it's not happening naturally and organically, there's a temptation to fake it. And of course, a book can't tell if you're cheating . . . so be honest with yourself and make a quick check: are you getting more volume simply by shouting? Remember – don't just listen to yourself, *feel* it. If it feels like it's hard work, then you're shouting.

   And what do you do if you *are* shouting? You can probably guess by now. Stop. Rest. Have a break, and come back to it in a bit.

While you're taking a break, there's one word of warning I'd like to pass on. Quite often you'll see people drinking as they speak. Before you knock back a refreshing Coke or iced water, ask yourself a simple question: would you take a cold shower after a long, hard, fast marathon and not expect your muscles to complain? Probably not. So why do the same sort of thing to your throat. If you need a drink, choose something tepid, or at least hold it in your mouth for a few seconds before you swallow it, to give it a chance to get closer to body temperature. Otherwise, no matter how good it might feel in the short term, it's just going to shock your throat (and perhaps also make it more likely that you're going to need to drink more, sooner).

Right then, I think that's the lot. If everything's working even approximately as it should, don't forget to enjoy it.

Before we move on – let's burn the house down!

This last set of exercises is something that I've been told was used by Marlene Dietrich. I've no idea if that's true, or even if it was useful to her if it was true. That said, it's a very good exercise anyway! Don't try it until you've got a bit of confidence about your *power* . . . or unless nothing else seems to work!

You'll need to get yourself a candle and a cigarette lighter. Matches are a bit too clumsy, given how often you're going to need to re-light the candle. The candle itself needn't be particularly big, but it does need to be a traditional (tall and thin) candle rather than a tea-light candle.

You might want to think about putting down newspaper (or something similarly disposable) to catch any drips of wax. If you're really nervous of the wax, it's useful to make a tight 'collar' for the candle (card is fine) to slip around it, so that nothing can drip down onto your hands.

The exercise itself goes something like this:

1. Sit on a chair, with your bottom perched right at the front and lean forwards over a desk. Make sure you aren't slouching.

2. Check that you're not in any draughts that are likely to make the candle's flame flicker. Take sensible safety precautions.

3. Light the candle and let it burn for a little while to settle down, and to burn up some wax. This is to give you a reasonable amount of wick and a relatively steady flame.

4. Establish your breathing pattern – do it pretty well as before, as though you were lying down, and then move your attention to the candle's flame.

5. Holding the flame relatively near your mouth, purse your lips and blow gently. You should be able to tip the flame over onto its side, but without blowing it out. In an ideal world, you would be able to get the flame tipped over by 90 degrees, but anywhere around 45 degrees is fine to start off with.

6. Hold the flame there for as long as you can with one breath.

You'll find that the only really easy way of getting the kind of control you need to be able to blow the flame *over* but not *out* and to *keep it alight* – despite burning at 90 degrees – is to use your diaphragm. You can certainly move the flame by using your upper chest to breathe, and with some practice you can manage to keep the flame tilted over, but at the very least you'll be able to feel that you're doing it. If nothing else, this exercise will reinforce your ability to tell what's from your diaphragm and what's not! Using your diaphragm muscle will mean you can keep the flame tipped over for much, much longer on fewer breaths than you could hope to manage using your upper chest muscles alone.

With just a little work you'll be able to keep the flame tipped over for quite a long time, with less and less flickering as you establish better and more sophisticated control of your diaphragm. Less flickering, by the way, is at least as important as the length of time the flame is tipped over.

A word of warning here! There's a bit of a risk with this exercise (apart from the obvious one of burning your house down!) which is that people sometimes get so hooked on holding the flame down that they either forget to breathe or gasp for breath at the very last second. The first problem is self-righting,[11] but the second is a bit more insidious. Gasping for air almost

---

[11] Eventually, your body will *make* you breath, whether you want to or not!

inevitably means that you grab the air into your lungs with your upper chest and that you tighten your throat/neck/shoulder muscles as you do it. By now you should have grasped that this is not a good thing!

Incidentally, from your body's point of view, using the top part of your chest to gasp in air makes a lot of sense in terms of the survival of the species! You can get the oxygen from your lungs into your bloodstream a bit faster that way and – as far as your body is concerned – that is a good thing to be doing, because when you gasp your body assumes that it's under some form of attack and responds with the so-called 'fight or flight' syndrome. In other words, it gets ready to fight whatever has stressed it – or to run for its life!

Once you've got used to using your candle, you can use it with sound, not just silent breath. You'll find this is a lot harder than you expect, but don't give up. Using the candle is an excellent way of doing two things at the same time:

- First, because we're visually orientated animals, you can concentrate on what you're looking at, and won't get so many hang-ups about the way you're breathing.

- At the same time, the candle gives you immediate and very obvious feed-back about how steady and prolonged your voice is becoming.

It may take a bit of time for you to be able to keep the flame tipped while you make a sound. Try starting with the open OOO sound (as in 'loop'), because the shape your lips need to be in is pretty similar to the ideal shape for flame-blowing (and for whistling). When you've got a bit of confidence like that, try some others, just for a giggle, but don't worry about getting them perfect because trying to keep your lips in a useful shape will limit how well you can make other sounds, such as an ongoing EEEEEE, for example. The reason for making other sounds is just to stop you getting too limited and associating the Ah sound with this exercise or even with this kind of breath control!

One last point before we move on. If using a lighted candle isn't practical for you, you can substitute tissue paper. A square of unquilted toilet tissue is the best. Hold it tightly along one edge (being careful not to tear it) between the forefinger and thumb of each hand just in front of your upper lip, so that it hangs down over your mouth, and see if you can move it in the same way as you'd move the candle's flame.[12]

You might be a lot safer doing the exercise this way, but generally I find it's not as good. Firstly, the tissue is heavier and so requires more work: secondly, it's harder to see without going cross-eyed, but thirdly (and most importantly), it's just not as much fun as a candle.

---

[12] With the obvious difference that with the tissue you're trying to move it up to be horizontal and not down!

3 Generation

Introduction – where does the noise come from?

Now that you've got more *power* to your voice, it's time to do something more with it. It's time to turn that extra energy into a better, clearer sound. It's actually easier than you might think. To get started, why not try one of the simplest of all exercises?

It's easy. Touch two fingers to the front of your throat and make a long S sound. Without changing breath, change the S to a long Z sound. Feel the difference with your fingers? The S isn't 'sounded' – it's just a hiss – so your throat is doing nothing, but when you start doing the Z you should feel your throat start to buzz. That buzz is the sound of the Z being made, down in your throat! Play with other sounds to see which of them are sounded, and which aren't. Just a word of warning – it's still best to do this kind of thing in private – unless you want to spend some time trying to explain why you seemed to be trying to take your pulse on your throat and hum at the same time!

You may find that you can't feel the buzz in your fingers (just like sometimes you can't find a pulse). Don't worry – feeling it in your fingers isn't as important as being aware of the buzz in your throat.

In fact, you may find that this whole section of this book is oddly and disappointingly short. That's because if you can feel the buzz at all, you've already done everything there is to 'do' in your throat – you're making a sound. The rest of this section is much more oriented to all the things that you *shouldn't* be doing in your throat. Things like –

- getting tense

- twisting

- blocking off the airflow

- getting sore

- interfering with the energy you create.

Actually, I've already cheated a little in this section. Much of the work for *generation* has already been done at the end of the last section. The rag dolls bit should have left you with your neck, and therefore your throat, in pretty well the right position for *generation* to happen.

Let me explain why. The essential point to remember about your throat is that you want to keep it open. (Well, obviously you want to keep it open, otherwise you couldn't breathe and you'd suffocate, but in this context I have a more specific meaning in mind.) By 'open' I mean that the flow of air from your lungs should be able to move completely freely, or as near as possible to this.

In section two, you put a lot of effort into getting more air flowing out of your lungs, so it's a shame to waste it by having problems in your throat. It's possible to undo all the good you've done to get better breath (more *power*) by choking it off with a constricted throat. That's why the exercises you've done up until now have all tended to use very open vowel sounds, particularly Aah. You didn't need to do much (or indeed any) work to get your mouth into the *shape* you wanted to create the *sound* you wanted. 'Aah' is a pure sound, created almost entirely in your throat.

By the way, if you've taken a break between sections of this book, it might be worth spending just five minutes going back over the troubleshooting bit of the last section. It's very important now not to constrict your throat – not only will it get in the way of all that extra *power* you're generating, but, worse still, the extra energy has to go somewhere. If your throat is constricted and won't let the air through, then you're going to end up with a fight between your diaphragm muscle on the one hand and your throat muscles on the other. Believe me, it's a one-sided fight that your throat can't win. The upshot is that you'll end up getting a tired throat and more frequent sore throats.

Don't forget, too, that if diaphragm breathing is new to you, you may find that it all becomes too much like hard work, and your body may give up on the idea of wanting to breathe properly in the first place.

So, let's assume that your rag doll worked well (or that somehow, by hook or by crook, you've at least found your body neutral position). In that case your throat is lined up correctly and won't be blocked by a kink or twist. All we need to worry about now are problems caused by your throat constricting itself. To show you what I mean, get yourself sorted out into body neutral, and then start a long Ah sound. (You may need to do this a few times to get the Ah to be long enough, because your body can't store up in advance the extra air you need to hold a long note. But if you gradually demand longer and longer notes from it, it can react and give more and more capacity each time.) Once you've got the Ah to last for about eight or so seconds – but don't worry if you're getting less, just do what you can – start the Ah in body neutral position and then turn your head as far as it will go to the left without moving your shoulders. Carry on with the sound and slowly turn all the way to the right.

As you move, keep a feel for your voice (this is one time when you can probably hear the difference, just by listening to yourself). You'll find that at both extremes – fully turned to the left and the right – your voice sounds slightly strangled compared to how it sounds when you're facing forwards and closer to body neutral. That's because turning puts kinks in your throat.

For most people the effect isn't as pronounced when they do the same thing by tipping their head forwards and backwards, but have a go anyway and see if you can feel the changes in your voice as you do it.

As a quick aside, it's worth mentioning that you shouldn't be surprised if just doing this exercise makes a significant difference to your voice. If you already had plenty of spare power that could be used for anything (including perhaps giving you a sore throat!) just getting your neck posture sorted out will often free up all that potential sound and let it out.

Position is important – but so is having fun!

So far it all sounds very simple. Now you've got your position and posture right, in theory all I should need to do is say 'Relax' and everything would be fine. However, trying to make people relax is the practical equivalent of an oxymoron,[13] so let's spend a bit more time getting it sorted out.

To show you what I mean, it's probably best if you're standing in front of a full-length mirror. Try and ignore your reflection until you've got yourself in body neutral. Now, without moving anything, look at yourself. Just look, don't move. Once you've got yourself fixed in your mind, grin at yourself, and watch your shoulders as you do it. If I were a betting man, I'd say that as your expression changed your posture changed – your shoulders probably dropped. (Don't bother trying it again, now that you know what you're looking for; too much self-awareness can be a pain in the neck, and the

---

[13] You know the sort of thing: 'military intelligence' or 'loose-fitting tights'.

chances of your forcing things to happen are too high.) Instead of having a second go, just stay where you are and drop your shoulders again. Yes, I know I said you've probably just dropped them, but in most people they can go further than they do the first time.

You're probably concentrating on your shoulders by now and you've forgotten to smile. Pull a face at yourself by sticking your tongue out and now – without any great fuss or preparation – start to say some of the open sounding words you were using earlier on:

Maarley

Baarley

Taarley

Faarley

Caarley

Daarley

Chaarley

Sound different? (Or better yet, does it *feel* different?) Don't worry if it doesn't, it just means that either –

• it does and you've not noticed

• you were already pretty relaxed

• you've not relaxed despite my best efforts

• you're a zombie or an invader from Mars.

Whichever way, it's probably a good idea to have just one more go at it, or to stop and have a break. (Have you noticed I don't suggest that you write to your friends if you stop when things aren't going perfectly the first time?)

Here are some other tricks that people I know have used to help them relax their neck and throat (and shoulders and back and . . .)

• Recite a nursery rhyme to yourself. Make sure it's one you can remember without too much effort. If you don't know any nursery rhymes, or are embarrassed doing this, try reciting the lyrics to a silly song (but don't sing, just repeat the words). The idea is to say something (anything!) in which you're thinking a little more about what you're saying than how you're saying it. The knack is not to *make* anything happen, but simply to *let* things happen. Besides, saying something as nonsensical as a nursery rhyme should make you laugh just a little. Don't pick something with a strong beat (particularly not a four beat!) that you will want to nod along in time to, but something with a bit of a pattern is fine.[14]

- Have an imaginary telephone conversation with a friend – preferably someone you're delighted to hear from – not your mother phoning to see if you are eating properly or your bank manager (unless, of course, you're the one person in the country who really is genuinely pleased to get a telephone call from the manager!).

- Tell yourself your favourite (clean!) joke. It shouldn't be a one-liner and under absolutely no circumstances *whatsoever* should it be a blonde joke: I leave it to you to infer what colour my wife's hair is. If you *do* tell a blonde joke, a mysterious curse will come upon you and you'll never have a good voice. Don't ask me why, I don't know. It's just one of life's little mysteries!

- Put the television on (have the remote control handy so you can turn it off when you're finished) and find some kind of chat show or documentary. Talk back to the person behind the desk. If you find a wildlife documentary, tell the narrator exactly what you'd like to do to the pesky cat next door if it comes near your precious petunias just one more time. Got the idea? Don't get too excited – just enough to be able to concentrate more on *saying* something than on *thinking* about how you say it.

- As an alternative to the above, put the TV on, but turn the sound down, and provide a brief running commentary on something you're seeing. Be as rude as you like.

The general idea is pretty obvious, isn't it? Do something (almost anything) that makes you feel good and that involves your talking without thinking about the mechanics of it and getting all hung up about it. Then go back to the Maarley and Co. exercise, and see if you can feel the difference.

Okay then, that's about it! See! I told you this section was ridiculously short. It's not about doing anything, just about undoing things! However, before we move on, I'd like to take a few minutes to explain all about Loud Baby Syndrome. It's not a recognised medical condition, it's just a term I made up to describe the set of ideas I'm about to give you.

Loud baby syndrome – how to cry!

Remember the days when your kids really were just tiny babies? (If you've not gone through this, just bear with the rest of us for a minute or two, please.)

---

[14]   And so, although it pains me to say this, Britney Spears is better than Eminem.

There are a few important bits and bobs that you might have noticed about babies. First, they're small. Second, despite this they can be incredibly loud. Third, they're focused almost exclusively on their bodies and are completely self-centred. They don't think 'I'm hungry, but Mummy is a bit tired, so I'd better wait.' Oh no! They think 'I'm hungry, and I want to draw attention to that fact so that I get fed.' And how do they attract your attention? With their voices.

Perhaps because of their pretty basic nature, they've got no hang-ups and inhibitions. There is no emotional baggage to get between what they want to do – make a noise – and the sound that comes out. The ratio of *volume-of-body* to *volume-of-noise* is pretty good! They have no built-up stress.

As adults, however, we've suffered the 'slings and arrows of outrageous fortune'[15] and so we have a memory which is chock-full of mistakes that we've made, problems we've had, insults we've endured and so on. Even if we feel (consciously) that we've totally recovered, the theory goes that our subconscious stores up just a tiny fractional bit of 'upset' each time something goes wrong for us. These tiny bits of upset gradually build up, and by the time we're post-adolescents we've got a huge stack of these things sitting in our subconscious and giving us stress.

It's this accumulation of stresses that gets in the way of our *true* voices. If you had no stockpile of tiny stresses you'd be much more open and relaxed about your voice, which would be better for it. Hence the silly exercises to help you drop your guard a little and make like a baby. Lots of this might sound familiar to anyone who knows anything about the Alexander Technique.

Now that we've got that out of the way, it's time to move on and see about getting all of this under *control*.

---

[15] Yes, it's Shakespeare! I figure it always pays to drag the Bard in somewhere!

4 Control

Basics – just what is it that you want to control?

Up until now, I've been telling you that the noise that you make in your throat was what we were interested in. As you've probably guessed, that was a bit of a white lie. What people actually understand – words – are pretty well entirely shaped in your mouth. As a quick example, put two fingers between your teeth, with the fingers on top of each other, to hold your mouth open. Now try talking. Even though most of your mouth, particularly your tongue and your palates, are still free to move, what you hear is more or less unintelligible. All you get are vague and unattractive noises.[16]

If you're still not convinced that your mouth is where the work is done, try whispering. One long and complicated sentence (try one from a text in the Annexe which concentrates on consonants) should be enough to convince you that even though you're not making any 'sounded sounds', it's still possible to get a pretty good idea of what you're trying to say.

The reason for this is that all that's created in your throat is the bare bones of the sound. An unstructured noise. It's actually turned into something recognisable by your mouth – particularly by the different shapes that you put your mouth into.

We can subdivide the mouth a little more, and say that the noise coming up from your throat is turned into different vowels by the shape and position of your cheeks and the (hard and soft) palates towards the back of your mouth. The front of your mouth is responsible for creating consonants, generally by the positioning of your lips (and tongue), particularly in relation to your teeth.

As a rule, consonants involve more work for your mouth than vowels do.

---

[16] Which for the life of me I can't think how to write down!

All of this is something of a generalisation (not to mention a simplification!) so don't get too hung up on it. For what it's worth though, the list below tells you a little about where different sounds are 'shaped', or formed into English syllables, in your mouth.

Types	Examples	Comments
Vowel-type	Ah, Oo, Eee	Most of the work is done in your throat, with changes in the position of your cheeks and lips making the difference between the different vowel sounds.
Plosives	Bh, Puh, Th	Pretty well all the work is done by your lips stopping the airflow and then letting it go again (explosively!).
Fricative	Fff, Vvv	All the work is done by your lips and teeth
Stops	T, D	Your tongue and soft palate do all the work.
Diphthongs	OH, OI[17]	Where the work is done moves as the combination of sounds progresses.
Nasals and other things	Nnn, Rr	Your tongue and lips do the work.

[17] As in 'load' and 'loin' respectively

While you were going through this rough list, you may have noticed that quite a few of the consonants came in pairs, one of which was 'voiced' while the other was 'unvoiced'. Do you remember that at the start of section 3 on Generation, I asked you to make a long S sound and a long Z sound? That's an example of an unsounded and a sounded pair. Both are made in more or less the same way, in terms of the position of your mouth (if you're interested they are technically called a *voiceless alveolo-palatal fricative* and a *voiced alveolo-palatal fricative*[18]).

By the way, there's no such thing as an unvoiced vowel, for the obvious reason that the sound for a vowel is made more or less entirely in your throat.

Don't worry if you got lost somewhere in this convoluted (and frankly boring) bit. None of this is particularly important at the moment, except to make it even more obvious that our basic PGC[19] model is a gross over-simplification of reality!

But you knew that anyway . . . right?

Anatomy – a bit more background

Your face, particularly around your mouth, has an amazing density of muscles. They aren't big – certainly nothing like the diaphragm muscle you use for breathing – but their sheer density make them capable of moving your mouth, lips, tongue and so on into an almost infinite set of positions.

It's the effect of those positions on the air that's flowing up from your throat that changes the sound you make. That's why people from different parts of the country (let alone the world) have different accents. They form their mouths and so on into ever so subtly different positions, with quite spectacular results!

For the technically minded, the particular bits of the sound you make that are built up and strengthened by your mouth are called 'formants'. As a basic rule of thumb, the stronger your formant development, the stronger any accent or dialect you will have, and the more idiosyncratic your speech will be. Remember something from way back towards the beginning of this book though – there's no such thing as a bad voice, and if you've got an accent it's as important a part of your character as the colour of your hair or

---

[18]   There now! Aren't you glad this isn't a *serious* book about speech!
[19]   My abbreviation for 'power, generation and control' – basically for no other reason than that it's shorter to type.

eyes. If you want to have a go at different accents, you need to change the shape you make with your mouth as you speak, to make it the same as the shape made by the people you're trying to imitate. That's a job for a whole different book, I'm afraid – or better yet, a personal tutor.

Back to the muscles around the mouth for a moment. Consider these situations:

- Before you play a complicated piano piece (say, one of the trickier Bach fugues) you have a quick warm-up for your fingers and wrists, and perhaps your arms as well.

- Before you dance the ballet *Swan Lake*, you make sure your legs are well warmed up and relaxed.

- Before you run in your local charity marathon you warm up, just as you would if you wanted to play a half-way decent game of football.

- Before you start to talk, you . . . ?

Frankly, I'm prepared to put money on the fact that not many people think about doing a warm-up before they start talking. But why not? You're dealing with muscles after all; muscles which, generally, are underused (and under-appreciated!) but which are capable, when working together, of making the most fantastic things happen. So think about it for a moment or two.

Now, don't get me wrong. I'm not suggesting that you need the equivalent of a full fitness warm-up before you have a casual conversation at a party, but if you're about to make a longish speech or address that *particularly* difficult class of teenagers just before Christmas, it might not be a bad idea.

I'll give you a few exercises in a moment, but first a word of caution. Remember I said that your facial muscles were, generally speaking, quite small? That means that they tend to get tired quite quickly compared to larger muscles, such as those in your legs. They get a build-up of something called lactic acid, which stops muscles working properly.[20] It's relatively easy to do an over-warm-up, pass the point you want to be, and start heading downhill again. You'll see what I mean when you do the exercises!

Exercises – let's get physical!

Pick a short piece of text, something that's quite easy and that you don't need to work at too much. I like to use texts that people are going to work with later on, to get them familiar with them, so if you can't think of a

---

[20]   This is true for all muscles except – fortunately for us! – the heart.

suitable piece of text, have a go at this one (it's not in English, so don't worry if you don't understand it![21]):

> *Tué Tué Marima*
> *Tué Tué.*
> *Tué Tué Marima*
> *Tué Tué.*
> *Abossum ta Ama Jaromah*
> *Tué Tué.*
> *Abossum ta Ama Jaromah*
> *Tué Tué.*

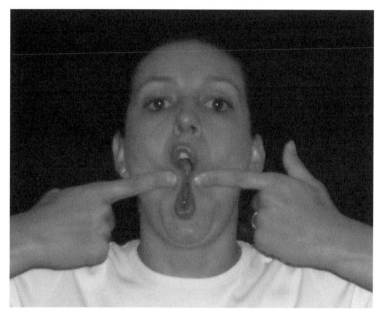

Figure 7

Here's the exercise. Read all the instructions through before you try it, as the different parts of the exercise should follow each other without too much of a gap for you to feel the effects most easily.

Say the text out loud a couple of times to get familiar with it, concentrating on how it sounds. Try and remember the clarity particularly, but don't make an effort to say it clearly – just use your usual speaking style.

Now, pinch your cheeks together by pushing on them with your fingers. Figure 7 shows you how. You'll need your teeth apart, so that you can push

---

[21] It's actually a Ghanaian song that means something like 'Move on, Marima, thanks to Ama Jaromah.'

your cheeks very well in – as far as possible without it hurting too much. You'll find that your lips make a crude kind of bow shape vertically and that your mouth is very tall and thin compared to normal.

Now recite the text. Your diction will be awful, because you won't be able to move your mouth properly. (The idea is to limit the movements you make in one direction, forcing other muscles to overwork to compensate, but don't worry about that, because it'll happen automatically.)

Concentrate on your mouth. You may feel a variety of things –

- your cheeks 'tingling' slightly

- a slightly disconcerting feeling around your nose

- an awareness of your sinuses

- your lips tingling

- a more 'alive' feeling in your face – perhaps even up as far as your eyes

- nothing, absolutely nothing.

If you do feel any of these, don't panic, they'll wear off very quickly, but in any case they're good things! If nothing else, you'll probably at least get a sensation of being more sensitive to the muscles in your cheeks and lips.

The second part of the exercise is the flip side of the coin. Put a finger from each hand into the corners of your mouth and pull your mouth as wide (and therefore flat) as it will go.

If you know the wide-mouthed frog joke, you'll be able to do this one with no problems. Now go over the text again.

You should feel similar things to the last time – perhaps with more likelihood that you'll experience the lip tingles.

Okay, now that you've woken up the muscles by making them work much harder than they usually do, take your fingers away from your mouth altogether and go over the text one last time. Pay really close attention to it, and see if you can feel how much more precise it is than it was the first time you did it (in your normal style).

Does is sound any clearer?

With a bit of luck, you should find that this last time through your diction is quite a lot clearer and more precise than it was originally. That's simply because your facial muscles were woken up by the exercise and so were working that little bit harder.

Before we go any further, stop and take a break. If you work too long on *control*, your muscles will get tired and not work hard enough to make a difference.

Here's another simple exercise that might leave you feeling less like a weirdo than the last one – but it is also somewhat less effective, I'm afraid. It is based on a short and simple piece of music as well as text.

For starters, pick a piece of music that you know well, and which is about the same length as your text (of course you could just use the verse of a song, which would guarantee that they'd be the same length). Read the text 'normally,' just as you did before. Then whistle your piece of music. Next, hum your music, making sure that you do it pretty loudly and that you press your lips together (in a kind of flat smile) as hard as you can. Lastly, speak your text out loud once more, and see if you can spot any differences.

A fun variation on this idea is not to have a specific short bit of music, but to try to whistle your text, so that you end up whistling something that has all the inflections and changes in dynamics and so on that you would have *if you were speaking*. In this version, you end up saying your text, whistling your text,[22] humming your text, and then speaking it again. The tempo, inflections and so on when you whistle it should be about the same as when you speak it.

You'll probably need a short break after this exercise too, partly to rest your facial muscles, but also to give you time to recover from how silly you felt in the last five minutes!

By now you should've got the hang of what I'm trying to do. And you've also probably realised that these exercises aren't much use in 'real life' be-cause you can't go through everything you need to say four times before you can say it in public! What's needed, then, is a set of short tricks and tips that will help you quickly freshen up your face before you start. (Of course, once you've got into the habit of working just that little bit harder with your face muscles, these tips won't be any more help to you.)

1. Yawn. I'm not talking about the polite little gestures you try and stifle when you're bored. I'm talking about the kind of fantastic, all-consum-ing, stretch-type yawn a cat does when it's getting ready to go out after a nap. Hold your mouth open for a good few seconds too.

2. Rub your face. Give yourself a quick massage. Do it like you're giving yourself a quick and vigorous refreshing wash. Concentrate on the area around your lips, particularly your upper lip (well, you don't really need to concentrate on that area, but I've found that people often ignore that bit unless I specifically draw their attention to it).

---

[22] Think of Po in the Teletubbies!

3. Smile a big, obviously false, manic-looking smile, hold it for just a couple of seconds, then change straight away to a cartoon-style kiss (lips ridiculously pursed, stuck well forward). Do this several times. Be careful not to over do it . . . and for your own sanity, don't try this in a room with mirrors!

4. Chew a huge imaginary bit of sticky, chewy toffee. Use big circular movements – you'll look like a cow chewing the cud, but don't let that upset you.

5. Practise a few tongue-twisters. The ones which work you hard in terms of consonants which are made at the front of the mouth (lips) are particularly effective. The traditional 'Peter Piper picked a pot of pickled pepper' is a great example, and you'll find others in the annexe too.

The point of all of these exercises is to do something with your face and mouth that is exaggerated and fully moves your face around lots. You can probably think of plenty of other things to do, most of which won't be nearly as silly as the ones I use, but don't forget that it helps if you find whatever you do ridiculous, or at least funny. That way you won't get too hung up about it . . .

. . . so long as you don't do any of these exercises in front of a mirror!

Reusing an old favourite – it's candle time again

I'm assuming here that this was a favourite exercise, but even if you didn't like using a candle last time, give it another go.

This time, instead of trying to hold the flame steady, albeit at 90 degrees from where it would usually be, you're trying to knock it about a bit. Before you used long vowel-type sounds and practised breath control; this time you're going to play with your lips and experiment with exactly how much work you can get them to do.

Before we start the actual exercise, here's a quick aside (and a silly exercise!). You'll be amazed at how much information you can communicate to people *just* by using your lips, particularly if you use sentences that have lots of consonants rather than vowels. Just for a laugh, pick a couple of sentences from the Annexe that are a bit more 'broken up' (that is, using lots of choppy consonants) than some of the others, and try saying them without using *any* breath at all.

If people are near enough, you'll be surprised to find that they can actually understand the bulk of what you are saying, even if you are scarcely making a sound. Why is this? Well, there's a general consensus that a lot of what people think of as 'listening' to other people speak is actually more a case of watching them speak. If a person's lips and jaw are in certain position, there's a fairly limited range of sounds they can be making. By putting that short list of possibilities into the context of what you know they said before (and after) you can make a decent guess at what they're likely to have said.

For a specific example, imagine you're at a noisy party talking to the new love of your life and you daren't show your age by admitting you can't hear them over the music. However, you *can* hear/see an explosive P sound at the beginning of a word. You can probably also hear the R at the end. At a guess, they're either saying the word 'poor' or the word 'pour'. By watching their lips between the P and the R you can make a pretty educated guess about which it is – although, admittedly, the difference can be quite hard to spot!

All of which explains why you can't lip-read cartoons.[23]

Okay, that's the aside dealt with, now back to what I should have been talking about all along:

1. Get yourself and your candle sorted out just like you did before.

2. Have a go at repeating the earlier exercise, just to get the hang of handling the candle again.

3. Do a sequence of really explosive P sounds, making sure that you don't breathe out after them. You want a nice clean 'P-P-P-P' rather than anything mucky like 'Puh-Puh-Puh-Puh'.

4. You should be able to make the flame 'bounce' on each P. Try it again with 'B-B-B-B' and the same thing should happen.

4. Try again with 'T-T-T-T' and the slightly harder 'L-L-L-L', 'F-F-F-F' and 'V-V-V-V'.

5. Lastly, just to finish on an easy one, do 'W-W-W-W'.

Got the image fixed? As you explode these consonants, the sudden rush of air moves the flame around. As before, don't get too hooked on one particular sound, but just play around and see what works. (You'll find that consonants that you sustain, such as MMMM, NNNN and SSSS, won't work.).

The aim is to see how far and how quickly you can bounce the flame. As before, the point is not to move the flame for it's own sake, but to stop you

---

23 The facial movements aren't animated in sufficient detail.

worrying too much about technique and at the same time to give you immediate feedback.

Incidentally, if you used tissue paper (toilet or otherwise) the last time
you did the candle exercise, you can do so again – and with the same
caveats.[24]

---

24 Which are basically that it's harder work and less fun!

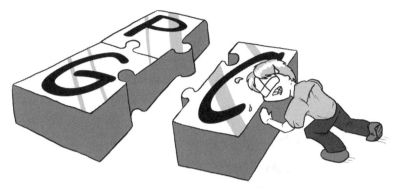

5 Putting it all together and stuff

Introduction – why we've done what we've done and what we're going to do next

So far all we've done is take the voice apart with our somewhat simplified PGC model, and concentrate on the three components individually. But that's actually running counter to the whole concept of what your voice is all about! It's a whole body thing, not a mechanical construct that you can take to pieces and rebuild rather like a poorly performing car. With a bit of luck, you won't have taken too much of what you've been doing too seriously, and so you'll still have a healthy regard for the sheer fun of using your voice. You may also have found that there's been quite a change in your voice already. For example, once you relaxed your neck and shoulders and started breathing from your gut (using your diaphragm) you may have noticed that your voice sounded somewhat lower and more woody (as opposed to tinny, for any of you Monty Python fans).

Now's the time we put things back together again, hopefully without forgetting any good habits developed along the way.

It's probably best taught (and practised!) by doing, so we'll work with some texts in this section (at the risk of this looking a bit like a 'serious' book on speaking!). At this point in the process, many voice tutors would direct you to the most fantastic poetry and take it apart to help you look at it in consummate detail and 'do it properly'. As you may have already guessed, that's not the style of this book!

I'm going to use some poetry, but not too much. This is for a couple of reasons, some more important than others.

- Good poetry is written to be read (aloud) so it's too easy!

- You might not like my taste in poems and get hung up on the poems themselves.

As an aside, however, I can't recommend strongly enough that you go away and play with some good poetry. If you find you like the examples I've chosen in the Annexe – such as Jack Mapanje's stuff – you'll almost certainly find that it's particularly rewarding to work on them out loud. (Maya Angelou, another of my favourite poets, was at one point an elective mute, who was induced to speak again partly through poetry.)

We're going to be using some famous speeches too, again, because they're quite easy to do out loud (after all, they were meant to be spoken, not just written and read in your head) along with a couple of bits and bobs of theatre text for the same reason.

However, the main things we're going to use – eventually – are harder and more realistic texts – the sort of things that you're more likely to have to read in everyday life (well, okay, you might not read a JavaScript manual in your job, but you know what I mean).

If things aren't making sense, try and bear with me for a little while and see if I manage to explain things better, but don't get hung up on getting things right. Just as there is no right voice – just your voice – there is no right way to read something out loud. There is just *your* way of reading it. (Which isn't to say that there aren't lots of *wrong* ways, of course!)

If you've tried the exercises a couple of times, and it still feels like I'm talking rubbish, move on and come back to this section later.

Well, that's the general blurb taken care of . . . now on with the actual *work*.

Advanced toys – talking rag dolls

Not satisfied with the traditional toys of yesteryear, today's kids want their dolls and so on to be all action – walking, talking, speaking. So we're going to upgrade our rag doll exercise.[25] Before we do this, you may find it useful to spend five minutes reminding yourself what the rag doll exercise was and making sure you can do it comfortably. The exercise we are coming to really is the key to putting things together, so it's worthwhile reading these instructions through a couple of times to make sure you know what you're trying to do, and spending a bit of time on it if you need to.

---

[25] Don't worry, we'll not go as far as imitating dolls that eat, cry and ask for 'Momma'!

Here's the tricky part.

1. Decide what your working sentence is going to be for this exercise. It should be something short, and simple, perhaps even just part of a sentence to avoid the risk of overdoing things. Pick something that catches your eye from one of the examples in the Annexe, but make sure it's one that I've said is easy.

2. Get into the head-down position of your rag doll. This time, though, put your fingers into your mouth in the wide-mouth frog position.

3. Keep your fingers in place as you unroll.

4. Just as you get to the point where your head is more or less in place, suddenly take your fingers out of your mouth and push your cheeks and lips together into the exaggerated kiss position.

5. When you finally arrive in your body neutral position, launch straight into your working sentence.

If you're lucky, you should find that everything works nicely. You may even find that everything works absolutely correctly!

Don't worry if it's a bit tricky, this is quite a hard exercise. One possible warm-up for it is to do the lip/mouth exercises first, then immediately do a rag doll. Your face should stay warmed up long enough to do your sentence without any problems.

Once you've played around with this exercise for a bit, you'll probably find that there are quite a few things that can go wrong. It's time for a quick check to see whether you're suffering from any of the problems listed below. They're quite common, so don't worry if you manage to collect a few of them. If you manage to get them all at the same time, take up Bingo!

1. Tension in the neck and nervousness about finding body neutral.

2. Tension in your shoulders – which may be raised.

3. Tension in your back – which may even be leading to restricted breathing.

4. Falling about laughing at how ridiculous you look and feel.

5. Not changing over from 'wide-mouth frog' to 'kiss' in time.

6. Forgetting your working sentence.

Numbers 4 and 6 we can just forget about. They're trivial. Problems 1 to 3, however, are a bit more of a nuisance. They're also all related – actually they're all more or less the same problem with different ways of showing itself. Fortunately, the way to deal with them is pretty simple.

As you unroll during your rag doll, make a point of breathing out, and letting your arms flop. Do it a couple of times without doing the wide-mouth frog bit, and then put your fingers back, making a point of keeping the same feel in your body, even though your arms can't just hang.

Remember what I said earlier about muscle memory? Try and hold the muscle memory of how it felt when you were totally relaxed and getting it right, so that you can recreate it when you put your fingers back in your mouth.

By the way, if thing are getting really difficult for you (and you've done the usual trick of stopping for a cup of tea!) try going back to lying down and put your fingers in your mouth to 'play' for a few minutes before trying it again.

Problem 5 is just a matter of remembering.

Once you've got the hang of this exercise – or even as something of an alternative to it – you can try doing the same thing, but this time balancing on the balls of your feet or on your toes when you go into body neutral. That way you stay more engaged with the exercise (no doing things on auto-pilot, please!) and perhaps a bit more alert.

The obvious next step is to change your working sentence into something slightly more realistic, and perhaps a little bit longer. This is where the texts in the Annexe really come into their own. Read through them, and choose an easy one for now. Pick one that you like. This will make it easier to memorise part (or all!²⁶) of it. Make sure it's nice and easy for *you* (I can't tell you which to look at – different people find different things easy). Take your time to pick and choose because there's no point in trying to work with something you don't like.

Can I take a quick aside about what to memorise – in terms of length, at least? It should be something that's coherent, so think in terms of a chunk at least. This is because we're moving gradually towards 'real life'. It shouldn't be so long that you trip up in the middle of it because you can't bring it straight to mind: you don't want to spend more time thinking about the words than about how you're saying them.²⁷

To be honest, this memorising is probably the hardest part about this exercise – you can't do this exercise with your hands out in front of you holding the words (or, worse still, looking down at the page, because your head position will probably be wrong). The only people who stand a reasonable

---

²⁶ . . . but only if you're confident; better to work on part of it than to struggle to remember things as you're doing the exercise!

²⁷ Eventually you will, obviously, but not just yet.

chance of managing without problems when they're reading it are musicians who are used to working from music on a stand, but even so I'd strongly argue that it's not a good idea. The really good news, however, is that you don't need to memorise it perfectly – if you make mistakes, who's going to know? It's just an exercise, after all!

The key problem here is that people often get worried about the text they're using. Don't! Forget about it. It's just a means to an end and if you can't find a piece you like in the Annexe, find one somewhere else (but look for things that are similar to the stuff I've included for you. Otherwise you run the risk of biting off more than you can chew, for the moment at least). Nervousness will almost always translate into tension in your shoulders and neck, and that's a *bad thing*.

Obviously, once you're confident working with simple, short texts, (or parts of texts) feel free to play with more difficult ones and longer ones. Perhaps I should say here (again!) that text (or whatever you're saying) can be difficult in a (depressingly wide!) range of ways. All that matters here are those bits and bobs that place extra demands on your breath (duration and control) and on your mouth area.

The first sentences are the problem ones. Your body is very good at responding to extra demands placed upon it – for example, when you get hot your body kicks in some pretty sophisticated cooling systems. What it's not good at, however, is anticipating that sort of thing. Even though you know you're about to walk into a very hot room, you can't get your body to start sweating until you're inside the room. Your body is essentially *reactive*. The same is true of any demands you make for extra air. It's impossible to get your body to start pushing more and more air through in the *expectation* of your needing it, but if you make artificial demands on it, it can respond.

It's not too different from sleep; even if you know you're going to be working through the night tomorrow, you can't sleep extra today to store up spare sleep. (It may feel like that sometimes, if you go to bed early and go straight to sleep, but that's only your body catching up on sleep you've *already* missed!)

Knowing that your body will eventually react doesn't help, of course, if the first thing you say is one-very-long-sentence-which-doesn't-give-you-any-where-to-breathe-or-rest-and-is-ridiculously-stressful-on-your-diaphragm-and-its-ability-to-provide-you-with-air-for-your-voice. (By now you shouldn't find that sentence a particular problem, assuming you're getting your dia-phragm control sorted out properly.) The trick is to stress your air supply *before* you need it. Song writers sometimes do this by having a short first phrase, a longer second phrase, a still longer third phrase, and so on until they can write very long musical phrases indeed, knowing that the singer will be warmed up and able to cope.[28]

How do you stress your air supply beforehand? Well, assuming that you can't structure whatever it is you want to say to give you a built-in warm-up, there are a couple of tricks that you can try.

- Before you start to speak, change your breathing pattern, so that the in and out cycles are longer. Concentrate particularly on longer out-breaths.

- Run several phrases together that would otherwise be done with a breath between them. Obviously you need to make sure you don't run together words that should be kept apart (the end of one sentence and the start of the next, for example), but don't automatically breathe in where you would normally (instinctively) do so.

- Use any introduction, as a chance to stress yourself. Even your greetings can be used if you're sneaky about it! For example, if it's a lecture you're giving, you could explain the subject of the session in one longer-than-usual-breath. For teachers, it could go something like 'Good-afternoon-6G-sit-down-please-no-in-your-normal-places-Wayne-get-off-the-chair-Tracy-leave-your-hair-alone-and-will-you-please-turn-off-that-mobile-phone -Today-we-are-going-to-talk-about-glaciers-no-not-the-mint-the-rivers-of-ice-that-shaped-much-of-our-landscape-I-thought-I-told-you-to-turn-it-off'. Insert the class of your choice!

Don't get too worked up about this if it sounds altogether too airy-fairy. If you do it a few times as an exercise, you'll soon get the hang of it and so won't need to be doing it (consciously) in real life. And don't get hung up on the word 'stress'. I'm not using the word to mean you've got to break sweat and risk indigestion; just to mean that you should place a bit of an extra demand on your system.

Don't worry, your body will cope. It's designed to.

Moving on – by moving back to earlier stuff

The next stage is sometimes a bit boring, but if you remember your visualisation tricks from earlier on, it's going to help.

---

[28] Schubert is a really classy example of a composer who does this particularly well. Pop musicians tend to get around the problem by only having short phrases all the way through their songs.

1. Get yourself sorted out into body neutral position.

2. Practise your working sentence.

3. Use your working sentence to turn light switches on or off, burn holes in the wall, close doors, etc. . . . whatever you used as visualisation aids in part two of this book, when you were working on power.

You may notice things going wrong at this point – they often do. To be honest, if you notice that they're going wrong (you've got tight shoulders, you're not breathing from your diaphragm, your throat is tight, or whatever), it's a pretty good sign. Honest! It means that you've noticed that things are going wrong . . . which in turn implies that you know what you should be doing.

If that's happening, great. Once you know what you should be doing you're 90% of the way there. If you relax, enjoy what you're doing and do it little and often, muscle memory will help and you'll get yourself sorted out fine!

You'll perhaps have spotted that I'm not telling you what it feels like when you get it right? That's because if you get it *really* right, believe me, you'll know. In any case, the whole point of this book is to help you get the best out of *your* own voice, and all I could do is tell you how it feels for *me*.

If you've not noticed anything going wrong, the options are either –

• it is, and you've not noticed

• it isn't and you're lucky

• it isn't and you don't need this book any more.

Whichever you *think* it is, take a few minutes to go back over the list of problems earlier (towards the end of part two), just to make sure.

The final stage is, of course, to extend your range of working sentences[29] by picking harder and harder ones. Eventually you should be able to make up your own sentences – and eventually, of course, to say instinctively whatever you want to. Play with things from the Annexe, but if nothing I suggest there grabs your attention, and you want to have a go at putting together your own working sentences, here are some guidelines.

• Make them fun, or at least not related to anything you find stressful. It's probably not a good idea to rehearse what you're going to say to the tax inspector you have to see tomorrow!

---

[29] . . . which by now, of course, can be paragraphs or even whole poems, rather that just a simple sentence . . .

- If in doubt, keep them short. You can always extend them or even just say them twice (or more!).

- Avoid complicated things like sub-clauses,[30] or anything else that means you have to concentrate on what you are saying, rather than just enjoying how you're saying it. That means that anything too intellectual is probably a bad idea.

- Steer clear of anything that you've heard other people say or sing. There's too much of a temptation to copy their style (perhaps sub-consciously). Madonna is bad, nursery rhymes are bad, letters to a friend are good.

Remember, too, that with each change in your working sentence, you should make a point of going back over old ground if you even *suspect* that things aren't working out as they should

Try and remember not to panic at this stage. You're trying to pull together quite a few things all at once, and it's to be expected that something will go wrong. If things go persistently wrong, think about going back to working on the problem on it's own, but remember that if it ever (and I mean *ever*) gets to be hard work or boring, stop.

Have a break and a cup of tea . . . don't forget that trying to figure out if you're doing it right is just a matter of sensitivity to your own body and how your sound *feels* (not sounds!).

Take two – an alternative way into things

Here's an alternative way of putting things together that some people find much more useful. I find it's a bit too 'hardcore' for my personal taste, but it can certainly be very effective for some people! Think of it as a form of revision of some of the earlier exercises – albeit one with a new twist – rather than a progression and you'll see what I mean.

Having said that, you should try using a prop for a while before you decide you don't want to have a go at working with it seriously. Part of the use of this technique is that it makes you aware of things you don't normally notice – which often makes you feel slightly uncomfortable. If you try it and don't like it, feel free to skip the rest of this section.

---

[30] A sub-clause – or anything like it – is something that you could put in brackets, or even take out, without serious damaging the flow of what you're saying. In this sentence for example, the subclause, *which you could easily remove*, is in italics.

The gist of using a prop is that instead of using your fingers to hold your lips in a restricted set of positions, such as the wide-mouthed frog and the exaggerated kiss, you use a prop to hold your teeth apart. A prop is anything that keeps your mouth open. Normally, when you close your mouth, your teeth rest on each other – the prop is simply something that sits between them to be rested on instead. If you want to do this *properly*,[31] you can buy professional props (traditionally made of bone, but now more often of plastic).

Before we go on, can I just mention that it's perhaps more sensible to make your own prop, rather than buy one. You want something that's not going to damage your teeth, but at the same time is going to be relatively strong . . . and obviously something that isn't going to pop out. My suggestion would be cork from a wine bottle. I'd also suggest that – unless you've got a mouth the size of the Channel Tunnel – you cut it down! Making your own has the added advantage that you can make a different sized one if you get to the point of wanting something bigger, and that you can cut grooves in the top and bottom to rest your teeth in, which will stop it slipping out when you squeeze on it.

The size you want to cut it to is pretty subjective, I'm afraid. It needs to be big enough to make you aware of the muscles in your face and jaw – by making them work in unusual ways – but not so big that it puts tension into them or, worse still, into your neck and shoulders. You'll have to experiment. If that means you have to drink several bottles of wine in order to get enough corks, then that's the price you have to pay! No pain, no gain, as they say.

Okay, once you've got your prop, it's useful to do some (or even all!) of the exercises you've done with your fingers over again. The prop will give you a very, very different awareness of your face, lips, mouth, jaw and throat. In the same way as making your face alive by rubbing it, or doing the wide-mouth frog and the exaggerated kiss, doing work with your mouth propped will make you sensitive to the movements of different parts of your mouth.

I've left using props until now because it's better if you can run through the previous exercises in relatively quick succession, and you need to be familiar with them to be able to do that. If you take too long over things, you'll lose the sense of progress and change that you'd otherwise feel.[32] So, as with more or less anything in the rest of the book, if you get tired, stop.

---

[31] Sorry about that, I just couldn't resist it!
[32] Besides, if you're anything like me, you don't want to have to deal with too many things at once. Pretty soon I'm going to try going for thinking and speaking at the same time . . .

Try and pay particular attention to two groups of things – perhaps by doing exercises more than once.

- First, the prop will allow you to be more aware of the positions of your tongue, jaw and, to a lesser extent, your soft palate. This is particularly important for getting the feel of vowels.

- Second, because it limits how much help your lips can be in making the sounds it will make you more aware of the work your lips and tongue do.[33] This is especially important when it comes to making consonants.

It goes without saying, though I'll say it anyway, that you should be careful when using your prop. Anything you put into your mouth that you can't chew and swallow is a potential choking hazard.

By the way, if making your own prop sounds too much like hard work, you can cheat by simply by putting two fingers – one on top of the other – between your teeth as an experiment. That way you'll get an idea of how much difference working with a prop *might* make to you . . . without the bother of making a prop, but at the added risk of biting your finger tips!

Before you try the next bit, you may find it useful to spend some time going over a number of working sentences – starting with easy ones – with the prop in place, just to make sure you cover a wide range of sounds (that is, mouth shapes).

Moving on – moving around

It's all well and good talking about all the stuff so far, but there's a crucial relationship between everything in your body, and one that I've tended to gloss over because I was trying to concentrate on the individual elements.

The relationship I'm talking about is the physical one between your diaphragm, chest, throat and mouth. Once you're in body neutral you've got it right. Or at least, that's the intention of the body neutral position! In real life though, you can't always maintain that perfect relationship. Remember the effect on your voice when you simply turned your head? Your voice sounded relatively strangled. In other words, your voice can be affected quite strongly by even relatively small changes in your posture.

Well, here's the point where you finally find out why I said earlier on that your voice was a whole body thing . . . from your feet up. There's a knack to

---

[33] The individual sounds that spoken words are built up from are called phonemes, by the way – think of them as being like syllables in written words.

maintaining your body neutral posture, and that's to use your ankles and knees (particularly) as a kind of shock absorber.

Try this simple exercise, which will help you to see what I mean (I hope):

1. Take off your shoes and stand on tiptoe.

2. Put your arms out sideways, horizontally from your shoulders.

3. Hold that position for a few seconds, and take the time to concentrate on how much work your toes are doing. You'll probably find that they're flexing and unflexing quite a bit in an attempt to keep you balanced.

4. Make it harder on yourself, but easier to feel the work of your feet, by staying as you are but now closing your eyes.

Feel how much work your feet are doing to keep you upright, even when you're just standing still? Unless you're particularly concerned about your height, you don't spend your whole day on tiptoe of course, so this exercise is an exaggeration, but the point is still valid.

Now do the same set of exercises but keeping your feet flat on the floor. You should still feel your feet working – though probably not as much. A good body neutral position will minimise the amount of work your body has to do, but if you're anything like me you will find you can't always stay in body neutral as you talk. Life isn't like that. And frankly, it shouldn't be either! Walking around, uneven surfaces, shoes and nerves will all mean that you can't stay in your wonderful, new body neutral position. So what to do?

Well, the knack I was talking about is to absorb the shocks and variations caused by real life in your ankles and knees. If you've ever been skiing, you'll remember being told time and time again by your instructor to use your knees to absorb shocks so that your body and head stay more or less at the same level. The idea is to help you see more clearly by protecting your eyes from being bounced around too much. When it comes to speaking, the physical principle is much the same.

Try this:

1. Get into body neutral and then hold a long constant, open Ah sound.

2. Listen to check it's as stable as possible, without flutters and so on.

3. Jump up and down as though you were skipping.

4. Notice the horrible variations in your voice as you take off and land.

5. Repeat points 1 to 4, but this time just walk. The variations are probably lessened, but still there.

6. Repeat points 1 to 4, but this time make a conscious effort to absorb the shock of landing by flexing your knees and then straightening them. If you're up on your toes as you jump, your ankles can help too.

7. Listen to the sound you make now, and compare it to the original.

You'll find this exercise can be surprisingly tiring, so don't go on for too long – otherwise you'll find that your voice has variations in it because you're exhausted, not because you are bouncing around!

If you want to make life particularly hard for yourself, try holding your open Ah sound as your go up and down stairs.

Clearly, real life is much easier than this exercise (unless you habitually try and talk to people while you're skipping). First, your body doesn't normally get this amount of jolting. Second, without thinking about it, you often structure the way you speak so that any jolts to your voice are timed to coincide with punctuation marks such as the end of a sentence, or when you'd normally break to take a breath (which, as an aside, is usually when you'd put a comma if you wrote your sentence down although there are other reasons for putting a comma – so don't feel obliged to breathe in every time you read one!). Once you're aware of this trick, you can use your knees to protect your voice so that you can say exactly what you want to say, not a slight approximation designed to avoid jolts.

If you combine this trick with the freedom you should started to get to make longer or more complicated sentences (which, of course, is the benefit of diaphragm breathing) you'll be amazed at how much difference it can make to the way you speak. You'll end up with a lot more flexibility in how you make up your sentences (or even paragraphs) and that will mean you'll end up with a potentially more interesting way of speaking – something less predictable and with more variation.

With a bit of luck, you'll now be able to make a decent stab at putting together some – or even all – of the things you picked up in earlier sections of the book. If not, don't panic! This is a good point to stop for a bit and take another look at how you're using your voice, because up until now, things have been part of an integrated model (PGC). The next section is a bit of a step away into new territory . . .

6 Resonance and stuff like that

What's resonance – am I a drum?

This bit's an add-on. By that I mean that up to now you were dealing with the blood and guts basics of your new voice. Now that you've got those sorted out, it's time to add a bit of a complication – which goes by the name of resonance.

And the short answer to that question is 'No, not quite, but you sometimes work that way.'

Resonance is what gives musical instruments their individual characteristics. It's why you might have heard of Stradivarius violins and Steinway pianos. They have a tone which is just that little bit better than the rest.

Resonance is (basically) sympathetic vibrations, which are a bit like good echoes. A good echo isn't one so big that you can shout a word at a cliff and half a second later hear the sound bounce back at you. No, it's one that's just big enough to amplify the original sound. Good tone comes from a kind of resonance which not only echoes back the original sound, but dampens out some bits and exaggerates others in such a way that the echoed sound is not only louder but also *nicer* than the original. The trick is to have the sound amplified in a hollow space, called a resonating chamber. The sound goes in, it sets up what are called sympathetic vibrations in the chamber, and the chamber's structure and shape mean that these vibrations (which is what sound is, remember) are augmented in a way that makes them sound even better.

Think about a violin for a moment. If you took away the sound box and just pulled a bow over the strings, without the hollow wooden bit behind it, the sound would not only be much, much quieter, it would also sound horribly tinny. Perhaps something like a horse's tail being scraped over the taught innards of a dead cat. Put the sound box back, however, and the richness of the instrument returns.

Think of your body like that. You make the sound in your throat (generation) but it gets amplified by the resonance chambers (empty echoey bits) of your body. Basically there are two such echo chambers – your chest and your sinuses.

A full, rich voice will use both chambers, although inevitably your personal balance between the two will be unique to you. Some people tend to have head voices (with predominantly sinus resonance) while others tend to have chest voices (with predominant resonance in the lungs). Here's a rough chart showing the general impressions people get when they listen to these different kinds of voice:

Type of voice	Resonating chamber	General impression	Examples
Chest voice	More resonance from the lungs than the sinuses	Emotionally rich voice with lots of personal sincerity associated with it.[34]	Pantomime baddies doing a villainous laugh (which is a good enough example of the sound, but not of the sincerity, obviously!).
Head voice	More resonance from the sinuses than the lungs	An intellectually reliable voice, with something intellectually important to say or something difficult to understand.	Anyone reading something that's not their own words – such as poor newsreaders.

Your throat is also a resonating chamber – obviously – but I'm not going to go into that here. You use it all the time, to make any sound at all, and the only thing you need to know about it is that you should keep it relaxed and

---

[34] Professional liars take note!

open so that you can get the best out of it that you can! I've gone on enough about that earlier.

Don't get the impression from the table that you can automatically tell what kind of a person you're talking to simply by listening to the kind of resonance they use. It's not that exact! There's also the complicating factor of pitch too. It's easier to hit higher notes (within your personal range, that is!) by using your sinuses as the resonating chamber, and vice versa. You might, however, get a reasonable clue about whether someone believes what they're saying, or is nervous about what they're telling you, if you notice that they start to use more and more of a head voice – one which resonates more in the sinuses than usual. Of course you've got to know someone's voice pretty well to be able to spot this!

Let's do a quick and simple test to see if I can explain what I mean any better when I do it practically . . .

1. Hum a long, sustained note, somewhere in the middle of your range – the pitch that you just naturally hum at. Try and make sure that the humming isn't sitting back in your throat, but is, instead, up at the front of your face, as if it were coming out between your eyes, at the top of your nose. Concentrate for a second on your mouth; can you feel your lips or teeth buzzing? That's the vibration caused by the sound you're making as the air flows out of your lungs and up out of your mouth (or nose if you have your mouth closed). Now, think about the bridge of your nose. Is that also buzzing?

2. Carrying on with your hum (breathing if you must!) put two fingers of each hand on your nose-bone and the top of your cheekbone, just below where the bone stops (for your eye to see out of). You should be able to feel the buzzing happening all the way up there too.

3. Rest your fingertips on the top of your head – scrub them around a bit to get them through your hair to touch your scalp pretty directly. Feel the buzz? All of these latter bits of buzzing have been because of the amplification of your basic buzz (the hum) inside your sinuses.

4. Do the same with your chest, by putting your fingertips onto your ribs, on the front, and near the top – probably somewhere around your sternum (your breastbone, which connects the upper ribs at the front). You may need to experiment a bit with this one, too.

It's possible, by the way, that you won't feel any buzz in one or the other of these places. If not, try humming louder to make it easier to feel/hear and try again. If there's still nothing, it might be because you're not using one or other of your resonating chambers. Well, that's a bit of a white lie, because you probably are making them vibrate, just not enough for you to be able to feel like this.

Before we move on to think about how to use the different chambers at different times (or even at all!), can we skip back to the drum question for a moment? One analogy which I've found helps some people (though it horribly confuses others) is to think of your chest as a kettledrum, and to think of your head (sinuses) as more akin to a side-drum or snare drum.[35] Both are useful, but for different parts of the beat.

Playing with different kinds of resonance

Now that you've got an idea of what your different resonating chambers are, it's about time we tried to play with them to see about making them work a little harder. This is quite a tricky set of techniques, so don't worry if you can't get the hang of them straight away. Just being aware of your options probably increases the likelihood of your making use of them. Let's start with head resonance:[36]

1. Get somewhere safe and private, then sing a loud, long note, somewhere in the middle of your range. Be careful not to get stress into your shoulders or throat.

2. Now stop and do it again, loud, like you mean it!

3. Keep that volume but slide up and up the scale, while you listen carefully to your voice.

4. Eventually you will end up going into a falsetto[37] voice but before that you'll find a point at which your voice 'breaks' and the way it's coming out changes – or at least it feels like the place it's coming out of changes. As a rule of thumb, once you get to that break point you're using only head resonance.

5. Get a feel for what head resonance is like. Concentrate on how it feels, rather than how it sounds. This is important.

---

[35] With the snare bit taken off!

[36] There are dozens of jokes to be made here about actors being airheads but I'm not going to stoop so low – honest!

[37] Falsetto is that weird kind of voice men use when they're doing bad impressions of old ladies.

When you're using your head resonating chambers, you'll be able to feel the vibration in and around your nose as you did before. If you carry on going higher and higher, you'll find that the resonance disappears. (That's a sign that you've gone too far and that you've probably actually switched to using a falsetto voice.)

There's an important caveat I should add at this point. Don't get the idea that, just because I used a high pitch to get you to use your head resonating chambers, it's only used for high-pitched sounds. It is often associated with them (particularly by singers struggling to reach the high notes of a piece!) but it's not an exclusive relationship.

There's no magical way to get access to your head resonance whenever you want it, so the exercises[38] here may feel a little odd at first, but if you've got this far you're probably used to that by now!

- Use visualisation: just imagine the sound you make coming up and out through the top of your head.

- Force as much air out as you can without getting the other problems that you've come up against already. This will push the sound up into your head.

- Play and experiment – you'll be amazed at how much you can learn for yourself by now. Just be careful to avoid working too hard and making mistakes or getting into bad habits!

And let's move quickly on to chest resonance:

1. Try the exercise you did before, this time going down the scale until you feel no vibration in your nose/face. However, this exercise doesn't work quite as well going downwards for some reason, and the same caveats as before apply!

2. Stand in body neutral position, with your feet slightly wider apart than usual if that helps. Make the (by now) usual Ah sound with your hands on your ribcage to feel for any vibration.

3. Make a conscious effort to relax your stomach muscles, then the muscles of your bottom. Relax them almost to the point that it feels like you need to go to the toilet.[39] Keep concentrating on your chest's vibration as you

---

[38] Just as a matter of gossip, this kind of exercise is used by men wanting to develop a more female-sounding voice – actors, cross-dressers and transsexuals included.

[39] Sorry . . . I've tried to explain this in different ways to various groups, but this is the way more people understand than any other!

do it. With a bit of luck you'll feel – rather than hear – the change in the tone of your sound as it is supported more and more by resonance from your chest.

4. Use visualisation – think of the sound you're making as actually coming out of your chest, quite low down, somewhere below your ribcage is about right for most people but experiment for yourself. Everyone's different, don't forget.

Much like working on your lips and mouth made you more aware of their potential, and that in turn made you more likely to use them more, just being aware of the possibilities of chest and head resonance will be very liberating for your voice. When you speak, don't try to make these resonances happen; the more you try the less it's going to work. But there are a couple of quick exercises you can try that will encourage you to use them more:

- Pretend to be a patronising, arrogant, uptight university lecturer who clearly thinks he knows lots more than the people to whom he is lecturing.[40] You'll probably find that you instinctively tend towards more of a head resonance – head voices are used to reinforce intellectual content.

- Pretend to be a woman (unless you're already a woman, in which case pretend to be a nervous, old woman). Make sure that you don't do it by tightening your throat and neck, or your shoulders.

- Say a difficult working sentence – one that you have memorised! – several times over, back to back, and quickly.

- Say 'I, I, I, You, You, You' perhaps with the I's higher in pitch than the You's. With luck, you'll slip into the habit of moving from head to chest as you do it.

- Pretend to be a really over-the-top villain in the style of Abanazar from the pantomime Aladdin . . . and laugh evilly as you get finally hold of the magic lamp. Nice and low, nice and evil, nice and self-indulgent.

- Recite some of the really good poems that are included in the Annexe – the one by Jack Mapanje is particularly good as it not only encourages you to open up and relax while you perform, as all good poetry does, but it also contains particularly earthy sounds.

---

[40] And just in case you were wondering, yes, I do have someone in mind!

The really important thing here is just to relax and enjoy yourself. Once you've got your posture sorted out and have started to have fun if you just go for it, things should really start to happen for you quite quickly and easily.

Don't despair if it takes longer to get yourself sorted out here than it has for other things. This is quite a subtle change we're looking at! At first, just being aware of the possibilities and potentials is all you can hope for – and maybe all you need is to let yourself go in any case.

7 Machines are taking over!

Personal beliefs – it's a matter of principle!

Much as I'd like to think your voice is all you need, the real world isn't like that, so it's probably a good idea to talk about the good, the bad, and the downright ugly! Or as the rest of the world calls them, electronic sound systems.

You can't expect me – an evangelist for people using their voices – to get all enthusiastic about microphones and systems with speakers, and I don't. The reasons I don't like them aren't entirely rational, I admit, and microphones do have their place: there are times when it's entirely appropriate to resort to using them and so on, but in general, and at risk of sounding like someone from Orwell's *Animal Farm*, there's something I'd like to make clear at the outset . . .

Microphones bad, pure voice good

Got that? If not, treat it as an exercise and repeat until convinced!

Okay, okay, I'm overstating the case massively, but at least I'm up front about my prejudice and you can keep it in the back of your mind while you read the rest of this chapter!

To be fair, perhaps I've just had bad experiences with non-professionals and microphones, but it seems to me that few things more quickly reduce an otherwise perfectly normal, intelligent person to the level of a gibbering idiot than a microphone. (A TV camera pointing at crowd of sports fans is about the only thing that may come close.)

With luck, this section will help you avoid most of the major pitfalls and – if not turn you into a natural – then at least help you avoid looking like the village idiot.

However, before we go any further and start looking at when, how or even whether, to use microphones, it's worth taking a quick look at how they – and the rest of a sound system – work.

So what is a sound system? – the nature of the beast

Any artificial system consists of a number of parts, just like your voice does . . .

- Input – the sounds that go into the system

- Manipulation – how the sound is modified (accidentally or deliberately) within the system

- Reproduction – how the sound is turned back into something that people can hear

. . . so I'm going to deal with those three sections in order. Don't panic if something doesn't make sense at first – a lot of this kind of stuff can *only* make sense if you *already* know everything else.[41] Read the rest of this through and see if it falls into place before you panic . . .

Electronic systems work by taking sound waves and using them to make part of the microphone move, just like anything else. This part of the microphone – called (confusingly) the diaphragm – converts your sounds into electronic signals. This is the input part of the process. These signals are then *amplified* by a piece of technology called an *amplifier* (who said scientists have no imagination, eh?) and the amplified signals are then fed to the speakers. This is the part of the process I'm calling manipulation. Speakers are just like microphones working in reverse, and they use the electronic signals to make parts of the speaker – the cones – vibrate. As sound is nothing more than a kind of vibration, hey presto, there you are, your voice coming out of a box! This is the reproduction part of the process.

While the signal is in its electronic form, it can be manipulated in other ways, too, not just to make it louder. It's possible, for example, to boost the bass (lower) parts of the sound, or boost the top end and take out the bass parts. As an example, just think of C3PO from Star Wars. I don't know for sure that the actor inside the suit didn't *really* sound like that, but it's certainly possible to make someone's voice sound like that by manipulating it.

---

[41] Like a lot of DIY kits, car maintenance instructions and computer software manuals!

By the way, manipulation of someone's voice like this is a pretty skilled job, carried out by a sound engineer. For the sake of this discussion, I'm just going to assume that a sound engineer is either part of the system that you don't control[42] or simply not part of your system.

Microphones come in a variety of shapes and sizes. Each of them has its own particular characteristics and its own personal best way of being used. Again, I'm assuming that the choice of what type of microphone to use is outside your control. However, they all have a couple of features in common:

- a pick-up range – the distance from the microphone that it can hear you in

- a pick-up pattern – the shape of the area around the microphone it can hear you in.

I'll cover what this means for you and your voice in a little while, but for now, just keep these two things in mind. Figure 8, which shows a slice through a pick-up pattern, should make things a little clearer for you.

Speakers are best thought of as microphones in reverse – at least in terms of what they do. And like microphones, different speakers do different jobs. The actual bit that does the vibrating (the cone – which you might never have seen because they're often hidden inside covers on home stereos) can, generally, only cope with a certain range of sounds. A very low note is best reproduced by a large cone (often called a woofer) and high notes can more or less only be reproduced from smaller cones (referred to as tweeters). One speaker may have a number of cones of different sizes to try and cover the entire range from very high to very low in one box.

So much for the nature of the system. Problems stem from the fact that all this converting to and fro isn't perfect. Some of the quality of the signal is lost in the process. (Technically, the signal is said to degrade or to get a poorer signal-to-noise ratio.) Put bluntly, speakers will always add some noise of their own to whatever you have to say,[43] although with good modern systems this is getting to be less and less of a problem. To add insult to injury, however, electronic systems also – generally – flatten out what you've got to say – and make it sound much more limited (because the conversions and so on aren't perfect). For example, if you've a particularly low voice and your system has only tweeters, your voice will sound tinny and unpleasant.

---

[42] To be frank, it's more or less impossible to control sound engineers anyway!

[43] Except for the system I heard at *Riverdance* on Broadway, but that's another story.

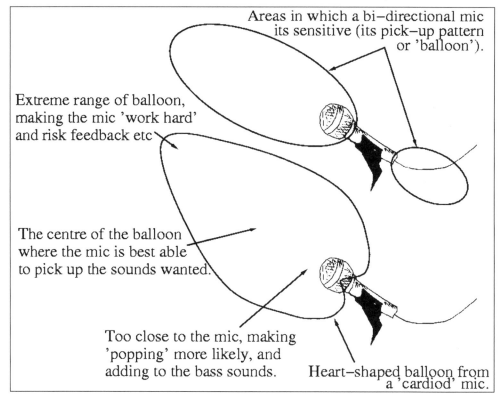

Areas in which a bi–directional mic
its sensitive (its pick–up pattern
or 'balloon').

Extreme range of balloon,
making the mic 'work hard'
and risk feedback etc

The centre of the balloon
where the mic is best able
to pick up the sounds wanted.

Too close to the mic, making
'popping' more likely, and
adding to the bass sounds.

Heart–shaped balloon from
a 'cardiod' mic.

Figure 8

If you've got a higher voice and only woofers, you'll sound unclear and indistinct. It's actually very expensive to create a system that covers everyone's voice fully – and therefore it's also particularly rare to find it.

If you're a bit confused by what I mean, just think of how tinny a person sounds on the telephone compared to how they sound in real life. Obviously that's a bit of an exaggeration, because almost any proper sound system is going to do better than that, but you'll see what I mean. Alternatively, think of how crass and creepy a lot of dodgy bingo callers and quiz masters sound; that's because they've taken out almost all the top end of their voices in an attempt to sound sexier!

One final word about this before we move on. Don't assume that just because your voice is being flattened, people will *notice* that it's being flattened out. Generally, your audience will think they hear what they expect to hear. Even if you decide to use your new-found abilities to go solo and not use microphones, they may not notice the improvement consciously . . .

. . . but trust me, it'll be there!

First things first – do you need the system?

That point brings me nicely to a discussion of when you use microphones and so on in the first place. Obviously, only you can judge whether or not to resort to an electronic system, but my preference is to avoid them like the plague, and only use them if:

- The place you're speaking is *very*, *very* big.

- Your words of wisdom are being recorded for posterity and you are absolutely sure that what you've got to say will bear the test of time.

- There are people in your audience (however you define that) who have hearing aids patched into some kind of induction system that needs input from microphones.

Now, obviously I'm not going to argue with the last one, but I'd ask you to think long and hard about the others. Have faith in yourself and trust your voice – you should be able to fill most spaces!

Don't rely on electronic help to help you overcome fears and nerves etc. I've heard people say that they can't project when they're nervous so they use some kind of electronic system to get over this. Rubbish! If you're nervous, you'll still sound nervous with an electronic system – but with all the added weaknesses of artificial systems added on![44] In fact, my personal experience has been the direct opposite of this, and I've found that using my voice properly has helped my deal with my nerves. The same goes for other problems – from lisping to stammering – which I've also heard people give as reasons for using microphones.

I've come across other reasons for people wanting to use microphones in the past too, all of them based upon the assumption that an electronic system is somehow magical. For the record, the kinds of systems you find in everyday life are *not* going to change –

- nerves

- stammering or stuttering

- tunelessness

- lisping

- strong accents

- colds, laryngitis, sore throats or whatever.

---

[44] Look, you've got to admit I did at least warn you I was biased!

That may sound obvious to you, but take my word for it – it's not obvious to everyone!

There are also other times when you're clearly better off not using a sound system. I suggest you work through this list of questions before you decide to turn on the microphones:

1. Is the system badly designed (or installed) so that there's lots of feedback (see later) or hum coming from the speakers?

2. Can I move around as I want to when I'm speaking, or will I be limited to one spot that I might not be comfortable in?

3. Does using the microphone mean I have to be in a location where I can't see the people I'm talking to as I'd want to? Is the microphone in the right position relative to my audience?

4. Would using a microphone make me look pretentious or annoy people?

5. Can I actually use the microphone properly? Is it positioned so that I can get close enough to it, or would I have to stand in the wrong kind of position? Is the stand the right type and height and in the right position?

Actually, there's something else you need to know about before you can decide whether or not to make use of a microphone-based system, and that's whether the system is designed to replace the sound of your natural voice or just to augment it.

Amplification vs Augmentation – that is the question!

The distinction between amplification and augmentation is a bit artificial, but it's useful for the sake of learning, so bear with me for a bit, okay? I like to differentiate between

• sound augmentation systems – or reinforcement systems

• sound amplification systems.

Both amplify your voice, so the names aren't particularly helpful, but the difference is in *how much* they amplify it, and how they play your voice back. Essentially an augmentation system is used where you just need a little-help-to-be-heard-at-the-back sort of thing. Systems like this don't do much in the way of amplification and you might even find that the sound coming out of the speakers is not noticeably louder than your own natural speech. The difference is that it's coming out of a speaker halfway down the hall, or whatever, and so it's effectively halving the distance between you and whomever you're trying to talk to.

You can't rely on an augmentation system to do the guts of your work for you, but – to my mind – they tend to be more true to your voice. People tend to get much, if not most, of what they hear *directly* from you, with just enough reinforcement from speakers to mean they don't have to strain to hear. There are no ways of getting proper figures for this, but my experience is that this is the kind of thing you're much, much more likely to find in churches, local halls, and civic theatres; you know the sort of place.

In the alternative type of system – used in places where you simply *cannot* be expected to make yourself heard without help – everything everyone hears comes from the speakers, and nothing is transferred to them directly from your mouth. We're talking about Wembley arena or a baseball stadium. To be honest, if you're working in the kind of environment where you need this kind of system, you're probably already too experienced to need any help this short book can give you.

It's important that you don't confuse the two types of systems. If you speak gently into a reinforcement system, expecting it to work hard (like an amplification system), you'll not put enough voice in for the system to work well, and you'll get a sound that's got lots of background hiss to it and can therefore be hard to make out properly. That's the most likely mistake for you to make, I think. Glance at the table to see what can happen if you don't treat a system like it's intended to be treated.

Type of system	How you treat it	What you get
Reinforcement	Reinforcement	The best combination!
Reinforcement	Amplification	Not enough sound for the system to work well
Amplification	Amplification	Something loud, but not very subtle[45]
Amplification	Reinforcement	Over-loud input or – at worst – distorted output

As a rule of thumb, it's better to assume that you're dealing with a simple reinforcement system, unless you've got evidence to the contrary. You've got a better chance of being right, and even if you're not, the consequences aren't as bad as making a mistake in the other direction.

---

[45] Not unlike my children, in fact.

Input – working with what you've got

I'm going to assume that you're not in charge of the sound system; either no one is in charge (it's just always been there, honest) or someone else is working it (as a sound engineer, or just as a dogsbody). Teaching you how to operate a sound system is outside the scope of this little book. Besides, you've got enough on your plate just dealing with what you *can* deal with – in other words, let's just talk about input.

Flip back through this book, and you'll find several references to making sure that what you're doing feels right, rather than sounds right. That's because you can never discover what you sound like to other people anyway. Well, that phenomon is doubly true when you're using some kind of sound system. You can't be in your audience and using the microphone at the same time (well, technically you can, but we'll talk about feedback and other reasons why it's not a good idea at all!). I'm afraid there's very little alternative to just doing your best and trusting the rest of the system not to let you down. You can only do so much by yourself.

You'll be using your voice and a microphone to make an input to a sound system. If I may, I'd like to start by borrowing an adage from computer programming:

Garbage in, garbage out

In other words, if you don't make the effort to put good quality sound into the system, what chance do you think there is of getting good reproduction out at the far end? As I've said, sound systems generally degrade the sound of your voice. It's possible – but not likely – that what comes out is better than what goes in, but you shouldn't bet on it. In the real world, the best you can hope for is that you don't *lose* any quality as the sound passes through the system. (I have heard a perfect system – once! – but we can't expect that your local church hall or school is going to have the facilities available for *Riverdance*.)

The obvious corollary of this is that you need to be sure that the quality you put in is the best you can manage. As a rule of thumb, the lower the quality of the system, the better the quality of your voice needs to be.

In terms of volume, too, don't assume the system will do your work for you. It's much easier for a system (well, basically the sound engineer if you lucky enough to have one) to turn you *down* than up. I'll try and explain the 'why' of that in a moment, but for now, just take my word for it – bigger is better!

Now, given that I've just suggested you want to get as much volume into the system as possible, you might be tempted to get as close to the microphone as possible. Don't. There's an optimum distance from the microphone, and getting too close will just cause your voice to sound distorted in some way (for example, your listeners may be able to hear you breathing or plosives such as P and B may cause a popping sound). Remember Figure 8, which showed the pick-up range and pattern of microphones? The key thing from your point of view is that you've got to position yourself within that space – which is often referred to as 'the envelope'. Think of it as a funny-shaped balloon being blown up by the microphone itself.

Actually, while it's true that there is such a thing as getting too close to the microphone, it's arguably more common for people to be too far away from the microphone – this seems to be particularly the case if the microphone is on a stand. Microphones don't bite,[46] so you can get close enough in perfect safety.

I'm afraid that how close you need to be to your microphone – like everything else about an electronic system – isn't something you can judge for yourself. You need to make sure you are speaking from inside the envelope and that, preferably, you're comfortably inside it, so that the microphone is working well within its tolerances.

The only realistic way to make sure you are in the envelope – beyond question – is to experiment. There's no alternative, I'm afraid, to trying out what you have to say in front of a microphone, with someone (who knows what they are doing and whose opinion you trust!) out front to hear how things sound.

Now, you'll have guessed (or if you haven't, I'm telling you!) that because of the shape of the envelope, both the angle of the microphone relative to your face and the distance away are important. To get the best position for the microphone, therefore, you need to test out every possible combination of distance and angle, with your friend telling you what sounds best.

Hmmm . . . nice idea, but far too time-consuming and ridiculously complicated. Rather, to get the best approximate position relative to the microphone, you can run through two simple exercises using easy sequences such as the alphabet or counting up from one.

1. Begin with the microphone a couple of metres away, and as you say each part of the sequence, move a little bit closer, until you're more or less touching the microphone with your lips. Your listener can then give you comments like 'it was strong between L and Q, but it started to get a bit fuzzy by the time you got to S or T'.

---

[46] Microphones don't, but I know a couple of sound engineers who probably do!

2. Once you've got the distance right, do the same thing, but this time, instead of moving closer to the microphone, change the height of the microphone (and it's angle, so that it's always pointing towards your mouth).

Here's a tip: an equally good alternative sometimes is to mix points 1 and 2 if you can, to make absolutely sure you've got the best position you can get. That is, change the distance a bit, then change the microphone angle, then change the distance, then change the angle, and so on. With a bit of luck you'll end up with both the distance and the angle sorted out very quickly.[47]

Incidentally, I'm not pretending that this simple system is foolproof. But it's better than nothing!

If you've only got time to do one or the other (that is, distance or angle, but not both) sort out the distance. Not only is it the most important, but you can probably make a good guess about the angle of the microphone – just aim it at your mouth. Remember though, that if you're in the classical position with the microphone on a stand in front of you (and lower than your face) you'll get a bit of a foreshortening effect – for the microphone to be pointing at your mouth, it'll have to *look* like it's pointing at your nose!

Using a sequence like the alphabet in all of this is an idea that works best for situations where you're under time pressure (maybe there's a lot to be done or other people want to practise). It's also good when your listener can't give you their opinions instantly – such as when you're practising in a church that's open to the public and you don't want everyone to hear their comments – especially if they're not flattering, or if (as is more likely!) your listener is shy about that sort of thing.

You may think that even this amount of testing seems a bit too complicated, but I'd strongly recommend it. At the very least you'll get some confidence in using the microphone as you practise! It doesn't have to take long or be any big deal. Just 30 seconds are all that's needed if everything goes right.

By the way, you should do your very best to say your sequence (A, B, C, D, or whatever) in the same way as you're going to be saying whatever it is that you're going to say when it's the real thing. The reasons are pretty obvious.

You might be tempted to use your actual speech (or reading, or whatever) as your sequence for your test. My advice would be not to, for these reasons:

---

[47] By the way, you can do these in either order – first distance, then angle, or first angle, then distance.

- Unless your friend is very quick on the uptake or knows what you're going to say as well as you do, it can be tricky for them to tell you how far you'd got when you sounded at your best ('Yeah, ah, it was fine when you were talking about clouds, but I couldn't hear much about the pain.' 'Pain?' 'Yeah, errmmm you said something about there not being any pain, didn't you?' 'You mean about the rain?' 'I don't know, sounded like pain to me.' 'Well, it could have been, I was talking about pain and about rain. Which bit was it?' 'How should I know? I couldn't hear it!').

- Doing something simple first often helps settle your nerves – the worst thing that can happen is that you make a hash of the piece in your practice.

- You can concentrate completely on checking the microphone if it's something as simple as the alphabet, because you don't need to think at all about *what* you're saying, just *how*.

- Running through a sequence means that you're more likely to speak in a fairly regular way. If you say something more interesting and variable, changes in how good you sound might have less to do with your position relative to the microphone and more to do with whether what you were saying was an easy bit or an exciting one.

- Sequences don't change, so you can double-check more easily than with something more interesting which – with the best will in the world – you'll never say exactly the same twice running.

By the way, all of this assumes that you're dealing with microphones that aren't the button type (called Lavalier microphones, technically). These are tiny microphones that clip onto your clothes and are almost always connected to the rest of the system by radio signals. If you're using a button microphone, the process is pretty similar – just practise and see what's best!

Once you've got the relative position of the microphone sorted out, the next thing you need to do is absolutely crucial – *ignore* it. This is a Golden Rule. Don't talk to the microphone – talk to your audience (even if that's just a couple of folk sitting at the back because they walked in by accident and the cleaner who's started to work early). If you start talking to the microphone, you'll not make any contact with the audience – either emotionally or with your eyes, and your body posture will be wrong. Worse still, you'll not work your voice properly!

There's just one possible exception to what I've just said about ignoring the microphone – and only one. If you're saying something that changes dynamic (how soft or loud it is) very suddenly, you might want to back off from the microphone just a little. Be careful not to get ambushed by changes that you don't notice; to you, the word 'protect' might be the same volume as everything else, but a very sensitive system might react to the plosive P and create a kind of popping sound. To be honest though, it's not a serious problem, and unless you're totally comfortable with microphones it's probably not worth worrying about – it's something of an advanced technique. To put it bluntly (and only a little facetiously) if the system needs you to move closer to and further from the microphone as you speak, it's such a poor system that you should consider doing without it altogether in any case.

Just before we move on – a quick warning about using microphones when you're reading something. Beware! Apart from the obvious problem of having a microphone in one hand (if it's that kind of microphone) and your text in the other,[48] the well-established law of Professor Murphy (from the University of Life) states that the microphone will pick up the sound of the paper shuffling and turning far, far better then you can possibly imagine. If you *must* read (I'm not a monster, I'll let you read anything that's longer than 32 sides) try and make sure that you position your mouth *much* closer to the microphone than the paper (even at the expense of having to read slightly more quietly because you're so close to the microphone). In other words, make sure that what you're reading from is not 'in the envelope'. That way you've got a better chance of not getting the sound of paperclips into the system! But don't go so far as to try and reach around with your arms and hold your text behind the microphone – you need to be able to see it to read it after all.

The best solution is a stand of some kind.

Feedback and other animals – the system fights back

Now, if all goes well, you'll never need to know anything about the wisdom contained in this next section, so feel free to skip it. If, however, you live in the real world . . . then at some point or another, you'll experience feedback.

Feedback is when the system gets its knickers in a twist, and starts emitting weird banshee wails. Remember that I said that electronic systems almost always add a little noise of their own? It's called speaker hum. Even when you're not saying anything into the microphone, if it's too close to the speaker, it will pick up the sound of that hum and feed it into the

---

[48] Just try turning the pages!

amplifier. The amplifier will do its job – amplify the sound – and pass that signal to the speakers. They in turn will do their job, and play the sound, but this time a little louder. The microphone will pick up this version of the sound and feed it into the system again. The loop will go on and on, and on, getting louder each time. It will only stop when you move the microphone away from the speaker (or the sound engineer, if there is one, switches the microphone off).

Actually there is another way it will stop, but as that involves expensive damage to the speakers, ear-splitting noise for the audience, and much embarrassment for you, we don't even want to think about it just now.

Now, to be fair, it would be daft to put a live or open microphone so close to a speaker that it did that. However, it can easily happen by accident, such as when a microphone gets dropped or is being moved around. Never, ever, on pain of death, pass a microphone from one user to another in front of a speaker. It's an easy mistake to make, but don't. Check for that kind of problem in your practice session.

The other way of getting feedback is much more common.

This can happen when you're speaking into the microphone – and the principles of the problem are exactly the same as I've just outlined. This time though, it's your voice that's getting picked up and fed around the system in an endless cycle. It's more common than the pure form of electronic feedback because once there is signal (that is something you want to hear – in this case your voice) coming out of the speaker, the size of the danger zone in front of the speaker is bigger. It tends to be a problem particularly when

- You're speaking into the microphone very quietly and the system (well, the engineer) has to turn the microphone's sensitivity right up to get enough input. This means that the microphone is now sensitive enough to pick up the sounds coming from the speaker, whereas it wasn't before. So long as you're right inside the envelope, this will be very unlikely.

But it might rear its ugly head in some other situations too:

- The system is set up for one level of sound, but you increase the volume of what you're saying, or someone else with a louder voice takes the microphone.

- The microphone moves as you speak – such as when it's a hand-held microphone, and you walk as you speak.

- You're speaking from in the middle of your audience and the speakers are a bit too close.

With a little common sense – and a quick look at where the speakers are before you start – you should be able to avoid this problem altogether. One quick, final word of warning . . . if you do get feedback, don't do the instinctive thing and automatically cover up the head of the microphone. It's very likely that your microphone isn't perfectly omnidirectional, but has some kind of cardiod pick-up pattern (see the earlier discussion about this shape of the microphone's pick-up pattern). If this is the case, and the problem stems from input into the *back* of the microphone (you'd be surprised at how often this happens) then covering up the input to the front – and therefore making the input from the back relatively more important – can only make things worse . . .

. . . sadly, I speak from experience!

Something you can't do much about, I'm afraid, is delay and echo. Bear with me for a second while I make an apparent digression . . . If the place you're speaking is so big that it needs you to use an electronic system of some kind, it's going to be pretty big by most people's standards. That means – particularly if the system you're using is a temporary one (or frankly, just plain bad) – that there will be a delay in your voice reaching the furthest parts of the building. If the building includes lots of open spaces and huge, flat stone walls and so on, you'll probably also find you've got a bit of an echo problem too.

Both these problems mean that people can't pick up what you're saying quickly or easily. Add to this the fact that in big buildings they can't see your face enough to lip-read (you'd be surprised how much they can infer from the shape of your lips), and you've got a bit of a problem. In short – if you've got to use an electronic system, you probably need to slow yourself down a little and work extra hard on your diction (making particularly sure that there are gaps between words and so on). See what I mean about this being a digression? You don't necessarily need to slow down because you're using an electronic system *per se*, but because of what that implies about the nature of the building you're speaking in.

Slowing down will do you no harm anyway – it's particularly good at helping with your nerves; and don't forget that you're always talking a good deal faster than you think in any case. Remember, too, that *you* know what you're saying[49] – your audience doesn't, so they have to think faster than you do, simply to hear what you're saying – and heaven help you if you expect them to think fast enough to *understand* it too!

---

[49] Which isn't quite the same thing as knowing what you're talking about, but close.

Pay attention at the back – checking out what you've picked up in this section

Time for a quick test, I think . . . some of these questions and answers are a bit of revision (so you needn't have read this section) but some of them offer a few additional tips.

Question	Answer
How close should I hold the microphone, or how close to it should I stand?	That's different for every system. If you've got time, experiment. If for some reason there's no chance to do that, remember it's usually less of a problem to be too close than to be too far away.
How do I find out what I sound like?	You can't – unless someone tells you.
If the building I'm speaking in, or the system itself, is so small or is set up in such a way that I can't speak without getting feedback, what should I do?	Stop using the system! If the space is so small you can't get the microphone far enough away from the speakers, what on earth do you need the speakers for in the first place!?!?
Do I need to change the way I talk when I'm using microphones?	In theory, not much, no. In practice, if you're in a space where you have to use a microphone, it's likely that you'll need to slow down a little and leave slightly longer gaps.
What's G.I.G.O.?	Garbage in, garbage out. Microphone systems can only work with what you give them!
What's the most dangerous part of a sound system?	It varies, but it's often the person talking into it.
What's a Lavalier microphone?	One that clips to your clothes, and passes your voice to the rest of the system by radio.
How do I figure out where I should be relative to the microphone?	Get some help out front and run through a simple sequence while changing position.

How do I test that a microphone is switched on?	Well, under no circumstances by tapping it or blowing into it! That not only makes you look like a jerk but risks damaging the microphone too. If you can't see the on button to check, say your first sentence; that way if it's open you'll not look daft by saying something like 'Is it on yet? Oh! Testing Testing!'
What is an envelope?	It's the three-dimensional area that the microphone can hear in. The size and shape are different for every microphone.
What happens if I speak too softly into the microphone?	Sound systems can only work with what you give them. Either you'll just sound too quiet to your audience, or you'll be turned up, risking getting a lot of hiss (or feedback) in the sound.
Is there a situation in which I should always use a microphone?	Well, if the space you're in is *vast*, obviously, or if you need to be heard by tape recorders or hearing aids.
If I'm reading from a book, what should I do?	Try and use the book as little as possible. Put it on a stand if possible, and make very, very sure that your mouth is more in the envelope than the book.

I think that about covers it – just one general point that's a kind of corollary to the Golden Rule. When you ignore a microphone, that means you ignore the sound you hear too . . . you can't hear what the audience is hearing, so it's even more important than ever to just go with what feels right and trust yourself.

8 And So On ...
or perhaps 'So What?'

Next steps – what do you do now?

This is the bit of the book that I've been wanting to write ever since page one. The rules for what you do now are simple – just enjoy yourself! Right back at the start I claimed that this book wasn't for dedicated, hardcore people – for voice professionals such as actors. It was for normal people in normal jobs. If you've got this far and you fancy your chances of becoming a voice professional, there are plenty of other books you can pick up. There's a list of some of them coming up. You could perhaps consider personal coaching too, or training as an actor, or whatever. Good luck.

For other people though, the option is just to carry on playing with your voice. Enjoy it, and remember that it's something personal and individual and unique. To return to the metaphysical stuff from part one, it's as special as you are. Relax and let it go!

If you're so fired up and enthusiastic you want to do more work, there are a number of possible ways to use your voice more:

- Increase how you use it at work – more presentations, better teaching, coaching or negotiating – or whatever.

- Make recordings for visually impaired people – books are useful, newspapers are (perhaps) even more so.

- Join your local amateur theatre company – though it helps if you can act too.

- Join a choir – there a thousands of small choirs all over the country, and singing is just an extension of what you've already learned.

- Get more coaching – there's nothing to say you can't become a voice professional too!

- Do some more reading. There's a short list of books listed below that should help.

For me though, personally, the most important use for your voice is the most basic and the most fundamental. It's to let out what's inside, to say what you've got to say, and to say it in a way that is truly and uniquely *You*.

Annexe: Sample texts

This is the hardest part of this book to write – without a shadow of a doubt! As one of my children would say, it's 'waaaaay tricky!' The problem isn't the obvious one of where to find suitable bits and pieces to include, but rather which to choose out of the myriad of examples that would do very nicely. The trick was to find things that you'd enjoy working with: there's no point in your trying to work with a piece of text that you hate – it'll just put your back up, and you'll end up thinking too much about *what* you're saying and not enough about *how* you're saying it.

Of course, ultimately, the idea is for you to be able to say things so naturally and freely that you only *need* to think about the content of what you're saying, but for now, I'm afraid things have to be the wrong way around.

In the end I gave up trying to second-guess what should and shouldn't go in, and just picked those things that I liked at the time. If you don't like one piece, try working on it for a bit and see if it grows on you. If you still don't like it after a genuine try, move on to something else.

Deciding what order these pieces should go in was almost as tricky as deciding what to include! There's no single right order – such as how hard the pieces are – because each piece has it's own harder and easier elements. Besides, each of them is interesting in its own right (well, to me at least!), and I've been suggesting to you that if something doesn't work, you should look at something else. That doesn't fit well with the idea of a hierarchy – which is what a formal order implies to me.

In the end though, I plumped for a very simple structure: I've split these examples into three groups – those that are good for giving your breathing a workout; those that are good for working your consonants; and those that are good at both. Up to a point, everything should be in the last group, but I've done what I could. Bear with me …

By the way, if you've fought your way through all of the pieces and you dislike enough of them to start to get the impression that I need my head examined, I've got some bad news for you: I'm afraid … what you see here was written *after* the therapy!

Breathing and getting your vowels

Here are a few example texts that I hope you'll find useful. I've put them – very roughly – into an order which matches how hard they are. It's important that you remember that everyone is different, of course, and so my order may very well not be your order. In other words, don't panic if you're struggling with a text; the next one might be easier for you!

Fishy Tales[50]

This is from a collection by Colin McNaughton called *There's an Awful Lot of Weirdoes in our Neighbourhood* – which is a book I've nicked from my children's bookshelves.[51] It's simply a bit of fun, but while you're reading it you might find that it's useful for playing with your breathing. It's an easy piece to experiment with. For example, you might want to do the whole thing in one breath; alternately, you might want to do it in two, breathing between 'fish' and 'My dad'.

> My friend Brian says
> that all the people who live in Finland
> have fins because they eat so much fish.
> My dad says it's not true
> but I think it might be.

By the way, you might also want to think about putting in the slightest break on the second line, just after the first word and another at the end of the third line. This way, you separate the things the Brian says from the rest of it. Another way of doing this is to change your resonance. Use head voice when you're citing Brian and chest voice when you're citing your Dad.

A nice easy piece ... and the person I know who 'does' it best is only eight years old.

---

[50]   "Fishy Tales" from *There's an Awful Lot of Weirdos in our Neighbourhood*, text and illustrations copyright Colin McNaughton, is reproduced here by permission of the publisher, Walker Books Limited, London.

[51]   . . . and if I could only remember which bookshelf it was, I'd put it back before I'm found out!

John: Chapter One, Verses 1–5

Well, I guess it was as inevitable as Shakespeare that there was going to be a part of the Bible in here somewhere, wasn't it? This is one of my favourite passages – even if I'm not sure I understand it properly! Here, though, it's included because it's so full of really good open vowel sounds. Try it early on (in part 2 or something): it's nice and short so it shouldn't be too hard to get good breath support for it, and the vowel work will always be useful. Don't get hung up about the consonants.

Similarly, don't get hung up on the actual text itself. If you don't understand it, or just plain don't like it, feel free to poke around in the rest of the Bible for similar passages. I don't mean similar theologically, just similar in terms of how much they open you out. You might like to play around with

Genesis 1–5

1 John 1–2

1 Kings 11

It's probably a good idea to steer clear of Revelation (too complicated!) and the long lists of genealogy in the Old Testament (too boring!). You might like to think about listening to what is read in church or on Radio 4 and see if you can find anything you'd like to try. By all means, feel free to play around and experiment!

By the way, my personal favourite, in terms of versions of the Bible is the New International Version (NIV) not least because of the way it translates this passage. The Good News version has a cute translation too. From memory, John starts something like this . . .

> **In the beginning was the Word, and the Word was with God, and the Word was God.**

And so on . . . whatever translation you use, this is a good bit to work with.

Not Like Today[52]

I have a confession to make here . . . I'd not even heard of Andrew Rumsey until I was working on this book . . . now, however, I'll make a point of looking at anything else he writes. There's great humour in the way he looks at the world, which makes me smile whenever I read one of his more witty poems, such as this one. I have to confess, too, that when I read it I can hear someone talking in a fairly strong Yorkshire accent, which makes me wonder who it is that this reminds me of.

From the point of view of a piece of text to work on, there are several ways of using "Not Like Today". Firstly, it's a great way of gradually expanding the amount of work you can do in one breath – and thus exercising your diaphragm. Start by only putting a line or two into each breath, but then work a little harder the next time you read it. Get to the point where you can go through a whole verse in one breath and you'll find that it's much easier to get an 'ideal' interpretation.

> cup of tea grandad?
> I'd love one thanks
> not that you can call
> it tea of course
> now in my day
> a cup of tea really was a cup of tea
>
> not like today
>
> slice of cake grandad?
> yes thanks love
> not that I'll be able
> to digest it of course
> they put so much rubbish in it now
> hardly seems like cake
> not proper cake like
> we used to have
> you knew where you were
> with a slice of cake then
>
> not like today

52 "Not Like Today" from *Homing In*, copyright Andrew Rumsey (Solway, 1998), available from Piquant, PO Box 83, Carlisle, CA3 9GR, UK at £1.99 per copy, plus postage.

the doctor sounded helpful grandad
doctors?
I could tell them
a thing or two
now in my day if
you were sick
you really were sick
and that was an end to it
rickets, dropsy, gout
proper diseases
with proper names

not like today

you'll pop by next Tuesday
won't you love
I expect I'll be feeling
more myself then

not
like today

A second way to use this piece is to do what you've just done, but in one verse! Instead of taking a number of readings through the piece to get to the state where you've got several lines over one breath, see if you can manage to do it almost instantly. Remember that your body responds to extra demand by being able to give you more? Well, this poem is the ideal way to experiment with that idea; start with just one line to a breath ('cup of tea grandad' and 'I'd love one thanks') then do two lines with your breath ('not that you can call / it tea of course') and then finish the verse off ('now in my day / a cup of tea really was / a cup of tea'). From the next verse onwards you'll be laughing – at least in terms of having enough breath to support your voice.

Finally, "Not Like Today" depends a lot on clear, tight consonants. Just try the last two lines of the first verse with deliberately sloppy consonants and you'll soon see what I mean.

Three things to look for in one short, fun poem. Excellent value for money, I think!

Wonderful Earth[53]

Wonderful Earth is a fantastic book by Nick Butterworth and Mick Inkpen. It was one of the favourite books my children had read to them at night when they were younger. I loved it so much that I suspect I read it to them for quite a long time after they grew bored by it! For me, a rich humour and joy of living shine right through this piece.

It was a standing joke that when we got to this page – we called it the list page – I'd go all out to see if I could do the whole page in one go; by one go, they meant doing it all in one breath. Once – and once only – I managed it: usually I'd go for three lungfulls, in the places marked√. Of course, I'm *not* saying that you've got to breathe where I do – or even that you have to breathe at all!

Obviously, I'm going to suggest that you use this extract to practise extending your breath. See how far you can get through the thing without having to take another gulp. By the way, you might expect that your second breath wouldn't take you as far as your first, because it was rushed or whatever, but you may be surprised as your body responds to the gradually increasing demands you're making of it. Your second (or even third breaths) might well be more useful to you than your first.

However, quite apart from the obvious test of seeing how much work you can get out of one in-breath, there's another use for this passage. The text is a really dense patchwork of different consonants and different combinations of consonants. A well-judged warm-up is the key to doing well here. Don't overdo it or you'll tire your lip muscles, but they do need a bit of preparation. A quick tip for the breathing exercise in the previous paragraph, by the way, is to have very, very good consonant definition – that way you can get away with using far less air on your vowels (it's cheating to skip them altogether though!) and you'll be able to get further than you thought possible . . . honest.

> √God made humming birds as small as bees and whales as big as busses, chameleons that can change to any colour, sloths that grow moss on their backs, parrots that can talk and swifts that sleep while they are flying, moths that look like leaves and insects that look like sticks, skunks that smell disgusting (except to other

---

[53] *Wonderful Earth* by Nick Butterworth & Mick Inkpen, Hunt & Thorpe, Arlesford, 1993. Extract reproduced by permission.

skunks), squirrels that fly, bees that dance, worms that eat mud and goats that eat anything, dolphins that smile, crocodiles that grin and hyenas that laugh, butterflyfish and parrotfish and lionfish and batfish and catfish and dogfish and hogfish, √hairy caterpillars and bald eagles, beavers that build dams and moles that dig tunnels, kangaroos that carry their babies in pouches and pelicans with beaks like shopping bags, sharks with teeth like razors, beetles with antlers, gorillas as strong as ten men, jumping fleas and jumping spiders, toads that blow themselves up like balloons, electric eels and beetles that glow in the dark, bears that sleep all winter long, termites that make tall houses tough as concrete, salmon that can swim up waterfalls, lizards like dragons, elephants with noses like hoses and squids that squirt ink.√ He made animals that sing and squawk and spout and hiss and hoot and howl and honk and chirp and peck and pounce and flap and fly and slide and slither and squirm and creep and crawl and growl and gallop and glide and dive and swoop and jump and hang and warble and squeak and roar . . .

. . . and he made the duck-billed platypus too!

Elizabeth the First, Queen of England

I'm a sucker for the big gesture. No matter how stupid something is, if it's done with enough style I get the hairs on the back of my neck coming up. I've always been partial to the story from World War II about a group of paratroopers on D-Day who chose to attack a well dug in and fortified German position wearing *not* their combat helmets, but their famous parachute regiment red berets. Why do that? Because they were *red* berets and the men of that regiment were suitably proud of them! Stupid, but stylish ... and almost certainly not a true story, but who cares!

Vocally, there are any number of speeches by men that raise the hairs on my neck, but not many by women, but this short extract, from Elizabeth the First, hits the spot twice over. It's a great speech by a woman and it's such a fantastic gesture.

I've included it here because it's a great chance for you to go over the top. Find yourself some time when you're not going to be disturbed and have a go at this piece. It's not a technical exercise this one, just something to really, really get your teeth into. As an exercise, it's just not possible to go too far. Close your eyes and imagine the nervousness and fear of your sailors, victory is by no means certain, and even if they win many of them will die, others return horribly maimed ... then remember that you're there to bring order to this chaos, and that deep in your heart, deep in your soul, you know what you are doing is *right*.

Imagine ... let it build up, and then do the piece again. But this time, do it *bigger*!

> ... and therefore I am come amongst you, as you see, not for my recreation and disport, but being resolved in the midst and heat of the battle to live and die amongst you all; to lay down for my God and for my kingdom and my people, my honour and my blood, even into the dust. I know I have the body of a weak and feeble woman; but I have the heart and stomach of a king – and a king of England too – and think foul scorn that Parma or Spain, or any other Prince of Europe, should dare to invade the borders of my realm ...

Magpies

This is a traditional little 'thing'. I don't know whether to call it a poem exactly, or a skipping rhyme or what, but whatever it is, it's quite a catchy short piece. You can do it lazily if you want to, but it's great practice for your consonants. As the lines go on, you'll get to make pretty well all the different consonant shapes at least once I think.

> One for sorrow,
> Two for joy,
> Three for a girl, and
> Four for a boy.
> Five for silver,
> Six for gold, but
> Seven for a secret
> Never to be told!

. . . and just in case you think I might know what it means – I don't I'm afraid, sorry.

Earthsea[54]

This is a choice that stems back to my own childhood. I got hooked on
Ursula le Guin at school and devoured the *Earthsea* series – about a wizard
called Sparrowhawk (whose real name I obviously can't tell you because
that would give you power over him!) and his adventures from rebellious
teenager through arch-mage to retired master wizard. One of the things that
captured my imagination was the language Le Guin used. The richness and
diversity of Sparrowhawk's world is somehow reflected in the richness of
the language – it sounds a bit arcane compared to contemporary English,
but probably not any the worse for that!

Before you try this piece for the first time, read it through to yourself a
couple of times. That way you'll get used to the patterns, and won't be taken
quite so much by surprise when you get around to doing it out loud. Normally I'm not a fan of 'reading in your head', but this time is an exception
because of the robustness of the writing – if you go with the flow it's great,
but if you're struggling or fighting against it, you will just be making life
harder for yourself.

From the point of view of using it as an exercise piece, it's worthwhile
spending some time and effort in looking at the number of open vowel sounds
that you need to get to grips with. The sentences aren't particularly long, but
they do tend to be slightly longer than you might use in everyday speech, so
that can be good for you too. Obviously there are plenty of consonants to
work at, but to be frank, there are other bits and bobs in this book that
should give you more of a workout in that field. Treat this piece more as an
exercise in producing good, clear vowels – with a little work on breath.

When he was done, he went back into the cave to the
boat, which lay prow forward, kept from the sand by several long driftwood logs. Tenar had looked at the boat the
night before, mistrustfully and without comprehension. It
was much larger than she had thought boats were, three
times her own length. It was full of objects she did not
know the use of, and it looked dangerous. On either side
of its nose (which is what she called the prow) an eye
was painted; and in her half-sleep she had constantly
felt the boat staring at her.

---

[54] Extract from *The Tombs of Atuan* by Ursula Le Guin (Gollancz, 1972). Copyright the Inter-Vivos Trust for the Le Guin Children, 1971.

Ged rummaged about inside it a moment and came back with something: a packet of hard bread, well wrapped to keep dry. He offered her a large piece.

It's quite an easy piece to work with, so you might want to use it relatively early on in your work. Having said that, sometimes it's worth coming back to a piece like this to see how much easier it's got for you and how much more robustly you cope with it (I hope!).

History Speaks[55]

The example I've chosen here is another emotive one, but one with a very clearly developed sense of quiet, personal dignity. It's not like the MLK speech, where you can (and for the sake of exercises *should!*) go over the top. Instead, it requires a much gentler tone, but one which has the same amount of self-confidence.

Make sure you've got plenty of support from your diaphragm before you make a stab at this one; you'll need to 'talk though' several places that tempt you to breathe in order to make the true sense of the piece obvious to the listener. For example, if you need to grab some air at the comma between 'character' and 'to vindicate', you'll almost certainly end up stressing the 'to vindicate' in a way that makes it sound like the start of a sentence. Here, the comma can almost be replaced by the words 'in order,' and I sometimes find it useful to mentally put that kind of thing into what I'm saying – it means that I pace the length of my comma-pauses better and that I hold in my head very clearly the meaning of what I'm saying. (It's a trick taken from reading stuff that's not written in normal, contemporary English, such as complicated poetry or Shakespeare, but it's useful in situations like this, too.)

> I rise as a minister of the King, and sustained by the just authority which belongs to that character, to vindicate the advice given to His Majesty by a united Cabinet – to insert in his gracious speech the recommendation which has just been read respecting the propriety of taking into consider-ation the condition of Ireland, and the removal of the civil disabilities affecting our Roman Catholic fellow-subjects. I rise, sir, in the spirit of peace, to propose the adjustment of the Roman Catholic question – that question which has so long and so painfully occupied the attention of parliament, and which has distracted the councils of the King for the last thirty years. I rise, sir, to discuss this great . . . .

In terms of resonance, you should make sure you've got plenty of chest resonance to make sure it sounds like you believe what you are saying (and

---

[55] The extract "History Speaks" come from *The Penguin Book of Historic Speeches*, edited by Brian MacArthur.

Peel, when he gave this speech, certainly got himself into political hot water because of it!). Having said that, the actual constructions used tend to be easiest with quite a bit of head resonance too, so you need to be quite well rounded in your tone to pull this one off well.

I'd suggest doing this one several times. First, go through it concentrating on your head resonance just to make sure that your intentions are clear. Then do it again, allowing yourself to go to town on your chest resonance. Fake that sincerity! Next, of course, you need to put both of these together. Be careful when you do this; it's very easy to lose both resonances when you try for a combination, and end up with an unbelievably flat and boring sound. That's particularly likely when you've listened to yourself trying it different ways, because your ear becomes jaded: make sure that you *feel* your resonance as well as listen to it.

When you're done, compare the quiet dignity of this text to some modern political speeches, just for a laugh!

The Tempest

It's about time for some Shakespeare. I love Shakespeare! Even after having studied him at school, I still love Shakespeare. Why? Well, frankly for all the usual reasons, not least because he writes a damn good story! At the moment, though, we're only interested in his writing – and for this example I'm going to pick on the Epilogue from *The Tempest*.

Some of my reasons for choosing this example are noble – to do with it being a good exercise piece – and some are less so. Amongst the latter is the fact that I once directed a performance of *The Tempest* in which Prospero (the lead character and a magician) was in a wheelchair. As he went through this Epilogue, he used a television remote control to gradually turn off the lights on the stage, one by one, until the last light, on him, finally went out as he said his last line. I thought it was a real tear-jerker . . . sadly the local press weren't quite so kind to the production.

Still, whatever my personal indulgences (writer's prerogative!), it's a good example of why you need loads of breath to support your speaking. Look closely at the text and you'll see it's bosh (sorry all you Shakespeare purists!) written in simple couplets. If you can't control your breath well, I'll make an even money bet that you'll end up taking a gulp of air at the end of one of the *physical* lines on the page. Unless you're lucky, though, that *won't* be the end of a sentence, and you'll have reduced the greatest English playwright of all time to a purveyor of dodgy rhyming doggerel! On the other hand, if you can control your breath so that you can breathe were you want to (or rather, where Shakespeare wants you to!) you'll have done his writing justice.

By the way, don't be nervous about taking on Shakespeare. He's well enough written that you can't do him any damage, honest . . . besides, as he's dead, he's not going to sue, even if you do!

> Now my charms are all o'erthrown,
> And what strength I have's mine own,
> Which is most faint; now, 'tis true,
> I must be here confined by you,
> Or sent to Naples. Let not
> Since I have my Dukedom got,
> And pardoned the deceiver, dwell
> In this bare island, by your spell;
> But release me from my bands
> With the help of your good hands.
> Gentle breath of yours my sails

Must fill, or else my project fails,
Which was to please. Now I want
Sprits to enforce, art to enchant;
And my ending is despair,
Unless I be relieved by prayer,
Which pierces so that it assaults
Mercy itself, and frees all faults.
As you from crimes would pardoned be,
Let your indulgence set me free.

Take some time to play with this piece of text. You'll find that as your breath support improves you'll be able to do more and more different things with it, and your effort will be rewarded, I promise. Don't do anything specific, just play and experiment.

Sorting out consonants and a bit of structure

There are eight examples for you here. They range from the very short to the relatively extended. Don't forget my comments earlier, that what's easy for me may be harder for you – and vice versa, of course! I bring my own personal baggage to each of these texts, and you'll have different baggage.

It's a Grave Business

This poem was culled from a gravestone in the area around Stratford-upon-Avon, in the south of England. It's not a particularly good example of the poet's art, but I didn't pick it for that. It's just a bit of an intro, to get us going, really.

> We loved her lots
> God loved her best
> And took her to
> Eternal rest.

See what I mean? It's not great poetry, but it captures somebody's thoughts about losing a loved one. Even for such an apparently short and simple piece, it's worth looking at, from our point of view. There's a particularly interesting combination of consonants – the D and the H – as in 'loved her'. You've got to be very careful not to let things just slide; if you do, you'll almost certainly lose the H and end up with 'loved'er' – probably all as one horrible sounding word!

Be careful, too, not to end up with a messy move between several of the other words, for example from 'God' to 'loved'. They're two separate words, make sure they stay that way.

You'll need to make sure you've done the wide-mouthed frog and the exaggerated kiss warm-up before tackling this. Make a point of keeping plenty of breath support and chest resonance – it's might be trite to you, but it was no doubt heartfelt. Try and treat it with respect. If you try hard enough, you can almost make this doggerel sound worthwhile!

When you're bored with that one, try this one – from a psalm, I think:

> For I will behold thy face in righteousness. I shall be satis-
> fied when I awake with thy likeness.

The first sentence is a bit of a doozy, consonant-wise. It's not a challenge to your breath control, so just treat it as an exercise in clarity. Try really hard to hear it 'fresh' each time you say it, because other people only get to hear what you've got to say once, and they don't have your advantage of knowing what you're saying: it's frighteningly easy to run words together in this extract because of the way the sounds are made. What does 'beholdthy' mean, or 'satisfiedwhen'?

Beatrix Potter[56]

I have to confess that I've never liked Beatrix Potter. My Dad was a fan and would use my brother and me as an excuse, I suspect, to read the stories himself. As a kid, I never quite got up the courage to tell him how boring I found them, and by the time I was an adult, I couldn't bring myself to burst his bubble. The irony of this is that now I've found myself reading *The Complete Adventures of Peter Rabbit* to my own kids, and being quite offended when they said they'd rather hear a bit of Harry Potter (again!). Don't get me wrong, I love the Harry Potter books and whenever a new one comes out there's always a fight to read it first – which the children inevitably win[57] – it's just that, frankly, anything begins to pall after the seven-hundred-and-twenty-fifth reading!

Having said all that, the earlier Potter, Beatrix, has pretty useful stuff. Here's a short – and very easy – extract from *The Tale of Mr Tod*. The sentences are nice and short, and even the longer ones have got breath marks (boringly called commas by English teachers, ha!) every now and again. Once you've become familiar with it, you can use it to start to explore how much spare breath-support you've got, by putting a couple of phrases into one breath.

> Benjamin Bunny came out of the dark tunnel, shaking the sand from his ears; he cleaned his face with his paws. Every minute the sun shone warmer on the top of the hill. In the valley there was a sea of white mist, with golden tops of trees showing through.
>
> Again from the fields down below in the mist there came the angry cry of a jay – followed by the sharp yelping bark of a fox!

While you're looking at these few lines, you might also like to take a bit of time to look at the consonants. There aren't many difficult combinations, so you can just have an easygoing play with the consonants themselves. In fact, the combinations almost seem to have been chosen to be easy (except for

---

[56] Extract from *The Tale of Mr Tod* by Beatrix Potter (copyright Frederick Warne & Co. 1912), published by Penguin Books, London. Reproduced with kind permission of Frederick Warne & Co.

[57] Actually, that's just what they think! What really happens is that I sneak back into their rooms after they've gone to sleep and read a few chapters before putting the book back, carefully positioned so that they can't tell!

'trees showing'). For example, moving from 'dark' to 'tunnel' in the first line is so simple because the K and the T are made by using different parts of the mouth. You can almost have the T prepared while you're saying the K, if you see what I mean.

Even when that's not the case, and the same part of the mouth makes two consecutive consonants (such as going from 'golden' to 'tops' in the last line of the first paragraph) it's pretty straightforward. All the letter N involves is closing your mouth with your tongue to force some of the air down your nose (pinch your nose while you say a long Nnnnnnn if you don't believe me), while the T is just a sudden opening of your mouth, pulling the tongue away from the position it's been in for the N. Neat, isn't it?

She Magazine[58]

To be honest, an example of this type could be taken from more or less any magazine of its genre. The point is that the sentences are short and sharp – nothing to put any stress on the amount of air you need to read them in one breath. What this type of piece does have, however, is a *lot* of consonant work. Read it over and see what I mean. It's a good starter piece in that regard. Nice and simple.

Of course, you might already be wondering what I was doing reading *She Magazine* . . . well, I was in hospital recently after an appendix operation and (to be frank) it's amazing how bored you can become sitting in a hospital. After a while, even daytime TV began to look exciting and interesting. I got to the point where it was either watch the *Tweenies* (again!) or read something that was lying around, and I got hooked! This particular example is from the March 2001 edition, from an article called 'The Lottery Wrecked My Marriage'.

> I was just 22 when I met Fiona. From the moment I set eyes on her, I knew she was the woman I wanted to spend the rest of my life with.
>
> We met in a nightclub. I was in the Army, based in Colchester, and was in Leeds on weekend leave. I couldn't believe Fiona was interested in me – she was gorgeous. But we instantly hit it off and started a long-distance relationship.
>
> After just three weeks, I asked her to marry me and she accepted. A week later she fell pregnant. It was all very fast, but we were extremely happy – Fiona was a couple of years younger than me, but we both felt sure we wanted to be together forever. I handed in my notice to the Army – I couldn't drag a family all over the country; I wanted to give Fiona and our child a sense of permanence.

As well as being built up of short, sharp sentences, this kind of text often contains plenty of opportunity for you to work on sentence structures that

---

[58] Extract from "The Lottery Wrecked My Marriage" from *She Magazine* (3/2001, p. 85) reproduced courtesy of *She Magazine* Copyright National Magazine Company.

are a bit more complicated – plenty of sub-clauses and so on for you to get your mouth around. In this example they're pretty easy, often just a single word (a name, for example) but it's a good starting point. The best way (for me at least) to deal with this kind of structure is to make a point of varying the kind of voice I use in the sub-clauses; I drop almost *any* chest resonance at all and just use a head voice for the (only intellectually important) details contained in the sub-clauses. Make a point of looking at other magazines – or newspaper articles – and you'll soon see what I mean (Mrs Jones, 50, of Acacia Avenue . . .). This article's a nice, simple, clean example.

Written to be read[59]

This is an extract from a press release. Like all (good) press releases, it's written in a particular style. The rules for this kind of text are based on the KISS principle (Keep It Simple, Stupid!) so that hard-pressed editors or journalists need to do as little work as possible to make it suitable for printing in their newspaper etc. In other words, it's got to be pithy and short, and it's got to 'pyramid'. Pyramiding means getting as much of the information as humanly possible into the first sentence and gradually getting down to the level of detail that most people aren't interested in towards the end. After all, people will more often read the start of an article than the end, and so an editor will generally start cutting from the bottom up. Press releases have also got to appeal to a wide variety of news media, so they'll tend to be written quite cleanly and in a fairly neutral style.

All of which makes them a potentially good source of material for easy exercises!

For a start, look at these paragraphs taken from a release put out by the Diana, Princess of Wales, Memorial Fund on 28 February 2001.

> As anti-landmine campaigners from around the world prepare to descend on Washington DC for a milestone event in the campaign's history, the Diana, Princess of Wales Memorial Fund – the organisation set up on the Princess's death to continue her humanitarian work – is ensuring the legacy of Diana, Princess of Wales, brings renewed support to the landmine cause.

> Through high profile visits to Angola and Bosnia in the last months of her life, Diana, Princess of Wales, did much to put the landmine issue on the map. She highlighted the terrible human cost to innocent civilians and the global extent of the problem.

> Much has been achieved since the death of Diana, Princess of Wales, including the introduction of the Ottawa Treaty banning the use, production and stockpiling of antipersonnel landmines. But the US and other crucial

---

[59] The press release in "Written to be read" was taken from the Web site of the Diana, Princess of Wales, Memorial Fund and is used here with permission.

governments are yet to ratify the global treaty, and land-mines continue to destroy countless lives.

The Nobel Peace Prize winning International Campaign to Ban Landmines (ICBL) is meeting in Washington next week . . .

Take a good look at this piece before you start reading it out loud. There are a couple of things that are worth remembering. In the first paragraph, for example, because the authors need to give you all the exciting information they can and set the scene with background information (such as what the Memorial Fund actually does) they have to rely upon sub-clauses quite a lot. Make a point of making them clearly distinguishable by using – say – a relatively pure head voice for the factual asides.

Another important aspect of this extract is the sheer importance in ethical terms of lots of what's being said; for example the civilians at the end of the first paragraph are *innocent* and at the end of the next paragraph the number of lives being *destroyed* (not just affected, but destroyed) is *countless*. Now, the piece as a whole is essentially a factual one and you might like to consider the balance between head and chest resonance to make yourself sound like an empathic newsreader (what you have to say is emotionally important, but you have to convey it in a way that's not over-emotional), but the key words I've just picked out probably deserve special attention. Stress them.

Of course, you can stress them simply by going louder, which is often effective, but can get tedious if you overdo it, or you can change your resonance balance as well.

Remember, I'm not saying there's a right way and a wrong way of doing this, just that you've got more options than you think . . .

The good news about this piece, though, is that there are plenty of places where you can breathe without damaging the sense of the piece, so you can use it both as an exercise in support and control early on in your development and as an exercise in subtlety later on!

Peter Piper

A good, old-fashioned tongue-twister. This one is particularly good for consonant work. Obviously the letter P gets a bit of a workout, but so do quite a few others.

> Peter Piper picked a peck of pickled peppers.
> If Peter Piper picked a peck of pickled peppers,
> Where's the peck of pickled peppers Peter Piper picked?

Be careful about working with tongue-twisters. You'll have guessed that I've included a couple here because they make you work very hard indeed with your consonants – do them slowly and concentrate on how your mouth feels as you do it. Don't try them at competition speeds. The problem, of course, is that the whole point of tongue-twisters is to tire out your lips and mouth, until your ability to speak properly collapses and the twister has claimed another victim. It's fun, but it's not a good exercise.

Here are a couple more tongue-twisters that you might want to have a go at:

> Dodgy van, dodgy van, dodgy van
> Dodgy van, dodgy van, dodgy van
>
> Red lorry, yellow lorry;
> Red lorry, yellow lorry.
>
> Chatter chatter chatter chatter
> Chatter chatter chatter!

And a particularly useful one – more of an exercise in consonants than a true tongue-twister . . . (and with just a little imagination, it's a perfectly reasonable test for your breath control, too):

> Knives and forks and spoons and knives
> And forks and spoons and pudding!
> Knives and forks and spoons and knives
> And forks and spoons and pudding!

You might (or might not!) want to know that that one was made up by my daughter on a walk while I was trying to calm her down after a fight with her sister. This last one has the same origins . . .

Willy the whale makes whopping waves.
Willy the whale makes whopping waves.
Willy the whale makes whopping waves.
Willy the whale makes whopping waves.

. . . and is obviously best done after you've warmed up your face muscles very thoroughly indeed – otherwise it'll just be a vague blur.

JavaScript[60]

JavaScript is a language for writing things that work[61] on the Internet. You're not going to learn programming here – I'm only interested in the language of the book, not the language of JavaScript!

This is a short extract from a book that tries to teach people JavaScript in 24 one-hour lessons, so it's very intense, with ideas very closely packed together. Technical writing of any kind isn't usually intended to be read aloud, and the authors are more or less universally interested in saying *specifically* what they mean, very precisely indeed, but without any thought at all to anyone who actually might want to speak it! Sadly, I'm afraid that all too often we are required to read out technical or scientific writing – even if it's just the instructions on how to assemble some flat-pack furniture!

For example, the World Wide Web is shortened, almost universally, to (helpfully) 'the Web' or (very unhelpfully!) WWW, pronounced Double-You, Double-You, Double-You. Something of a mouthful, even when you're used to it.

In general terms, technical manuals also tend to be pretty heavily scattered with consonants. When you read over the couple of paragraphs in this example, just have a look at the sheer density of tricky words. 'Language' isn't an easy word, nor is 'capability' – they're both quite hard work. Even the 'Although' at the start of the second sentence is tricky to say out loud; not because it's got so many difficult consonants, but because it's so easy to be lazy and indistinct with words like that . . . there isn't a consonant at the end (well, there is, but it doesn't sound) so it's actually difficult to know when the word stops! What's even worse, the next word starts with a short I sound – it's very easy to make this ugly, by making it into a kind of vague, imprecise, glottal, generic vowel. If it's tight and precise, you can use it as a proxy for the end of the last word (by making the start of this one clean).

> The World Wide Web (WWW) began as a text-only medium – the first version of the HTML (Hypertext Markup Language) specification didn't even have the capability to include graphics on a page. Although it's still not quite ready to give television a run for its money, the Web has come a long way.

---

[60] Extract from *Teach Yourself JavaScript in 24 Hours* by Michael Moncur is published by Perarson Technology Group and is used by their kind permission.

[61] . . . and quite a few that don't!

Today's Web sites can include a wealth of features: graph-
ics, sounds, animation, video, and sometimes even useful content. Web scripting languages, such as JavaScript,
provide one of the easiest ways to spice up a Web page
and to interact with users in new ways.

The first hour of this book introduces . . .

See what I mean about the sheer density of consonants – and of combinations of consonants. If you're ever in the unenviable position of having to
make some kind of presentation using other people's technical jargon, it
pays to work very hard on your diction, particularly your consonants.

Style Kills[62]

I'm a bit of a rock music fan on one hand, and on the other hand I can get very excited about obscure and sophisticated classical music – some of it pretty inaccessible and bizarre! Robert Palmer's sophisticated rock music is a handy halfway house for me . . . and no, it's not an oxymoron, honest!

Having said that, Palmer himself describes this as the 'hardest rock thing I've ever done. It still gives me chills.' I've not included it here because of the music though (obviously!); it's here because of the lyrics. A lot of rock and pop music seems to rely on hard-working consonants rather than open vowels. I guess it might have something to do with the advent of microphones – I don't know. In any case, this piece just doesn't 'do' anything at all unless the consonants are clear and precise.

There are some particularly tricky combinations here. Even the first line, for example, means you have to do some pretty fancy footwork with your mouth (so to speak) to get the 'd' at the end of 'brand' and the 'n' at the start of 'new' clearly separated without sounding artificial. The trick is to work your lips and tongue so fast that you've actually got time to put in a slight gap between those words . . . but beware, if you're not working quite hard enough, people will become aware of the gap, *as a gap*, and you'll end up sounding like someone doing a bad imitation of the Queen. Clarity between words is a particularly difficult thing to achieve in this whole piece all ways around . . . which of course is why I picked it!

The bits of alliteration within lines will make you work just that little bit harder too. Just enjoy the 'music' of them and don't try and fight it.

> I see you got yourself a brand new bag
> You had enough of the imitation drag
> Although you're leaping to the latest thing
> You can't ignore the suspicion of a hollow ring
>
> Big Bills
> Cheap Thrills
> Style kills
>
> You say you set your standards way too high
> So you convincingly effect a compromise

---

[62] The lyrics of "Style Kills" are taken from the album *Addictions Volume I* (Island Records ILPS 9944), and are reproduced here by kind permission of Mr Robert Palmer.

Some unsuspecting body's gonna pay
When you discover that you can't always have your own way

Big pain, big pills, style kills
If he won't you will style kills

A word of warning is probably in order here. Unless you're listening and concentrating, you'll risk slipping through this piece thinking that it's easy, just because you don't notice the places where you could do better. For example, look back at it, and ask yourself, honestly, if you got both Ts at the end of 'latest' and the start of 'thing' in line three. And what about clarity between 'you' and 'will' in the last line – did you run them together a little without even noticing? This piece is a great exercise!

Putting things together

Now here's a tricky section to put together! Don't think of this as a definitive group of texts chosen because they fit together; instead, think of them as simply the miscellaneous group that was left over when I'd sorted out the other groups!

After Wiriyamu Village Massacre by Portuguese[63]

Jack Mapanje is a fantastic poet – one of my favourites. He's a really strong, gutsy writer, with lots of powerful open sounds from the vowels he uses, which fit perfectly to the strength of the things he writes about. If you're at all interested in poetry with a political (small P) edge, this is an author for you. Trust me, if you only buy one book of poetry in your life, this is one you should seriously consider.

I first got exposed to his work by accident. We were on holiday with friends and Tim and I had turned the TV on early to make sure we didn't miss *Star Trek*.[64] Instead we caught a BBC 2 programme that included an interview with Mapanje and a reading of some of his poems. It was simply stunning, and as soon as we got home I phoned the BBC to find out more about it. I'm afraid I could tell them nothing more about what I'd seen than what I've just written here, but (bless 'em!) they had no trouble at all in figuring out what programme I'd watched, putting me through to the right production office, and even giving me a list of shops near me that stocked Mapanje's work.

Now, after a build-up like that, this had better not be an anticlimax . . .

> No, go back into your exile, go back quick.
> When those Portuguese soldiers abducted
> Falencha's baby quietly strapped to her back
> And scattered its precious brain on Falencha's
> Own maize grinding stone, when those solders
> Grabbed and hacked Dinyero's only son
> With Dinyero herself stubbornly watching

---

[63] "After Wiriyamu Village massacre by Portuguese" is taken from *Of Chameleons and Gods* by Jack Mapanje, published by Heinemann. It is reproduced here with their permission.

[64] You have to understand – it was the second part of a two-part episode featuring the Borg! Some things are important.

Or when they burnt down Faranando in his own
Hut as he tried to save Alefa his senile wife –
Where, where was your hand? Tell me that!
And if you helped Adrian Hastings report
The Portuguese atrocities to humans, where,
Where is your verse? You have no shame!
No, go back until our anger has simmered.

No anticlimax there, I think! Be careful when you work on this; it's hard not to get wrapped up with the emotions of what's going on, but don't let your emotions interfere with your voice . . . or at least not until and unless you can control them (rather then be controlled *by* them).

Apart from stirring your soul, this poem has two uses as a voice piece. First, the lines/sentences are quite short, and you can use this piece to get some realistic practice in terms of breath control. However, you'll soon get the hang of that, and then you'll probably find that the piece works well as a way of encouraging you to have really strong, open, powerful vowels. (Ultimately, of course, you'll be able to use it for consonant practise too – and as a performance piece if that's what you're into.)

I Have a Dream

Surely everyone knows – or at least has heard of – this speech by Martin Luther King Jnr. It's a piece I've used for several years in workshops now, and probably will for a long time to come. It's fantastically emotive, not just for the obvious reason of its inspiring content, but also because of the way it's put together.

I'm not saying that MLK thought about these things consciously when he drafted it, any more than Bach thought about some of the beautiful maths of his fugues,[65] but if you just take a look at the section I've chosen (the famous bit from quite a way into the speech) you'll find –

- clear and open vowels matched to ideas which are also intended to be clear and open

- few – if any – painfully tricky combinations of consonants making it hard to get your lips in place in time

- some quite complicated sentences with lots of sub-clauses for you to practise with (which for me is a great example of my belief that you don't have to compromise the structure of what you say in order to make it understandable – so long as you've got a good voice to say it with!)

- some paragraphs which, even though they contain only one sentence, are quite long for a single breath. You need to be able to handle them comfortably and at a reasonable volume if you're going to do justice to the way this piece should sound.

> I am not unmindful that some of you have come here out of great trials and tribulations. Some of you have come fresh from narrow cells. Some of you have come from areas where your quest for freedom left you battered by the storms of persecution and staggered by the winds of police brutality. You have been the veterans of creative suffering. Continue to work with the faith that unearned suffering is redemptive.
>
> Go back to Mississippi, go back to Alabama, go back to Georgia, go back to Louisiana, go back to the slums and ghettos of our northern cities, knowing that somehow this situation can and will be changed. Let us not wallow in the valley of despair.

---

[65] Ah, the advantages of a classical musical education!

I say to you today, my friends, that in spite of the difficulties and frustrations of the moment, I still have a dream. It is a dream deeply rooted in the American dream.

I have a dream that one day this nation will rise up and live out the true meaning of its creed: 'We hold these truths to be self-evident: that all men are created equal.'

I have a dream that one day on the red hills of Georgia the sons of former slaves and the sons of former slaveowners will be able to sit down together at a table of brotherhood.

I have a dream that one day even the state of Mississippi, a desert state, sweltering with the heat of injustice and oppression, will be transformed into an oasis of freedom and justice.

I have a dream that my four children will one day live in a nation where they will not be judged by the color of their skin but by the content of their character.

I have a dream today.

I have a dream that one day the state of Alabama, whose governor's lips are presently dripping with the words of interposition and nullification, will be transformed into a situation where little black boys and black girls will be able to join hands with little white boys and white girls and walk together as sisters and brothers.

I have a dream today.

I have a dream that one day every valley shall be exalted, every hill and mountain shall be made low, the rough places will be made plain, and the crooked places will be made straight, and the glory of the Lord shall be revealed, and all flesh shall see it together.

I suggest that you play around with this piece of text several times as you plough your way through the rest of the book. It's got everything, and you can always find something in it to come back to and work on. You've got to remember though, that no matter how long you work on it, and how well you do it, you're never going to do it *right*. Why not? Well, because you didn't write it. MLK did, so – to borrow some computer jargon – it's optimised for *his* voice, not yours.

If that doesn't make much sense to you, go back and reread bits of the philosophy right back at the start of this book. The important thing to remember is that because your voice is unique, the way you *use* it is also unique; you will subconsciously pick words, phrases and combinations that your mind thinks work best for your voice. That means that a speech that sounds right for one person can sound simply awful if someone else gives it.

I probably ought to add that because this is a particularly long example, you don't need to be able to do the whole thing from memory. I'm afraid that I simply couldn't decide where to cut: even with such a long excerpt as this, you still don't fully get the power of the speech as a whole, but I had to cut somewhere!

Elections won and lost – sort of![66]

The two relatively short extracts that I cite here come from the speeches delivered by the winner and the loser of the U.S. presidential elections in 2000. I've put them both in because – in terms of voice exercises – there's relatively little to chose between them, and this way I can avoid offending anyone (although it's probably too late for that, now!).

First, the words of Vice-President Gore, conceding defeat on 13 December 2000:

> Just moments ago, I spoke with George W. Bush and congratulated him on becoming the 43rd president of the United States, and I promised him that I wouldn't call him back this time.
>
> I offered to meet with him as soon as possible so that we can start to heal the divisions of the campaign and the contest through which we just passed.
>
> Almost a century and a half ago, Senator Stephen Douglas told Abraham Lincoln, who had just defeated him for the presidency, 'Partisan feeling must yield to patriotism. I'm with you, Mr. President, and God bless you.'
>
> Well, in that same spirit, I say to President-elect Bush that what remains of partisan rancour must now be put aside, and may God bless his stewardship of this country.
>
> Neither he nor I anticipated this long and difficult road. Certainly neither of us wanted it to happen. Yet it came, and now it has ended, resolved, as it must be resolved, through the honoured institutions of our democracy.
>
> Over the library of one of our great law schools is inscribed the motto, 'Not under man but under God and law.' That's the ruling principle of American freedom, the source of our democratic liberties. I've tried to make it my guide throughout this contest as it has guided America's deliberations of all the complex issues of the past five weeks.

---

[66] Extract from speeches by Al Gore and George Bush on 13th December, 2000, are reproduced by kind permission of iCan.com

> Now the U.S. Supreme Court has spoken. Let there be
> no doubt, while I strongly disagree with the court's decision,
> I accept it. I accept the finality of this outcome which will
> be ratified next Monday in the Electoral College. And to-
> night, for the sake of our unity of the people and the
> strength of our democracy, I offer my concession.

Before you go on and look at Bush's speech, just take a moment to look at the lengths of the things Gore has to say – he starts off with short sentences that are a full paragraph in themselves, and gradually gets into the flow, so that by the end of this extract (and even more so in the rest of his speech) he is using longer, more complicated sentences and paragraphs. In other words, he's allowed his body time to catch up with the increasing demands for breath that he's making on it.

Now look for a moment at an extract from President-elect Bush's speech, taken from quite a way into what he had to say:

> I know America wants reconciliation and unity. I know
> Americans want progress. And we must seize this moment
> and deliver.
>
> Together, guided by a spirit of common sense, common
> courtesy and common goals, we can unite and inspire
> the American citizens.
>
> Together, we will work to make all our public schools ex-
> cellent, teaching every student of every background and
> every accent, so that no child is left behind.
>
> Together we will save Social Security and renew its prom-
> ise of a secure retirement for generations to come.
>
> Together we will strengthen Medicare and offer prescrip-
> tion drug coverage to all of our seniors.
>
> Together we will give Americans the broad, fair and fiscally
> responsible tax relief they deserve.
>
> Together we'll have a bipartisan foreign policy true to our
> values and true to our friends, and we will have a military
> equal to every challenge and superior to every adversary.

Together we will address some of society's deepest problems one person at a time, by encouraging and empowering the good hearts and good works of the American people.

This is the essence of compassionate conservatism and it will be a foundation of my administration.

Bush's speech is particularly interesting as an exercise for your voice. It's something of a clarion call to action and is therefore loaded with clear open bell-like vowels and so on – 'together' is a best done as clearly as possible – almost ringing like a bell, it's that sort of word – but there's plenty of tricky technical stuff to get your mouth around too. 'Medicare' and 'bipartisan', for example, are two of the least 'natural' words I've ever come across, at least in terms of how they sound when spoken out loud.

In short, these two short extracts from speeches have a few interesting things for you to look at and work on. You need to combine good vowel work from your diaphragm (without using your throat, just keeping it open), staying relaxed in your shoulders and back and so on, with exceptional work from your face and lips. Great exercise – even if they aren't great speeches!

By the way, when you're playing with both these bits of text, it's important to remember that they were spoken by people who (I hope) are very different from you: be careful not to try and do an impression of either of them – do their words in your own way.

Prometheus Unbound

Remember what I said about gestures when I was talking about Elizabeth? Well, don't think it applies to futile gestures like Scott heading for the South Pole. He was just plain stupid!

However, out of that stupidity grew a film which spawned a soundtrack that, when performed apart from the film, is called the "Sinfonia Antarctica" by Ralph Vaughan Williams. To go with the performances, the composer specified short extracts to be read before the different movements. If my memory serves me correctly, he also specified that they were only to be read at live performances, but the record sleeve in my vinyl collection has them anyway – that's how I was first introduced to this amazing piece of work.

When you read this out loud, make sure that you've got plenty of breath to spare, over and above what you think you'll need for the lines themselves. Simply by having it there, you can use it to give extra emotional weight to what you're saying. Crucially, you'll need to keep your vowels very open. If you close anything down – by having a tight throat, for example – you'll not only find that your throat gets tired very quickly, but you'll limit the sound. To echo a landscape as open (and as beautiful!) as Antarctica, you need open (and beautiful!) sounds.

Having said that this piece is essentially to work your vowels, it's worth remembering that with longish and open sounds (for example 'woes which hope') you need to be extra precise about your consonants and how you break up your vowels. Otherwise you'll end up with something which might sound amazingly like the wind moaning over the ice, but doesn't mean anything . . .

> To suffer woes which Hope thinks infinite;
> To forgive wrongs darker than death or night;
> To defy Power, which seems omnipotent;
> To love, and bear; to hope till Hope creates
> From its own wreck the thing it contemplates;
> Neither to change, nor falter, nor repent;
> This, like thy glory, Titan, is to be
> Good, great and joyous, beautiful and free;
> This is alone Life; Joy, Empire, and Victory!

This is from Shelley's *Prometheus Unbound*, and to do it justice you need loads of emotional support (breath!) from your diaphragm and chest resonance: you'll need to keep some head voice in the mix too, to stop it sounding self-indul-gent and overly messianic.

I'd suggest reading this piece out loud four times every time you look at it (although obviously not if you're just starting this book!). Read it once 'nor-mally'; then again making a meal of the vowels – exaggerating them; then again working very hard at the consonants – you'll end up like a poor imper-sonation of Noel Coward – to warm up your lips and tongue, etc. Finally, do it a fourth time, putting everything together, and compare it to how you said it all the first time around. If it's not better, you're either as good as you're going to get or, more likely, you need a break before trying again!

If you're really wanting to put yourself through the mill, or looking for a performance piece, do it an extra couple of times concentrating on your chest and head resonances, but don't try this until you're very comfortable with everything else.

Further Reading

Books which make great practice

- *Let's Go Home Little Bear* by Martin Waddell and Barbara Firth (Walker Books, 1991; Candlewick Press, 1993) is one of those books that make you wish you were a child again so that someone could read it to you! It's a beautifully simple book, in which two bears (Big Bear and Little Bear, funnily enough!) have a bit of a conversation. I use it in groups to practice chest resonance and head resonance.

- *Jesus' Christmas Party* by Nicholas Allan (Red Fox, 1993; Doubleday, 1997) is another book for children that's just fantastic for adults too. It's short (only 30 small pages, with only a few lines to a page), with great pictures, and the main character's build-up to losing his temper is great practice for loosening yourself up and working on your diaphragm breathing and chest resonance.

- *I Shall Not Be Moved* by Maya Angelou (Virago, 1990; Bantam, 1991) is a selection of poems, each one different and each one powerful. It's worth looking at them all, but in particular try the poem called 'Equality'. Treat it as an exercise in over-the-top-ness. Go for it, then turn it up and go for it again. And again . . . and again.

Books which are more technical

- *Voice and the Actor* by Cicely Berry (Virgin, 1991) is a fantastic book for taking things a couple of steps further. Cicely was the voice coach for the Royal Shakespeare Company, and so everything she does is based on that. If you seriously want to work on your voice with acting in mind, this is an excellent next step.

- *Away with Words* by Sue Page (Lynx Communications – SPCK, 1998) has one chapter on voice, but it has other chapters on an awful lot of other useful things too. It describes itself as 'A training book on the whole spectrum of Christian communication', so if you want to use your voice as part of a Christian ministry, you could do worse than have a look at this.

- *Clear Speech* by Malcolm Morrison (A & C Black, 1989; Heinemann, 1997) includes a nice diagnostic section to help you deal with particular bad speech habits. It focuses more on positioning the lips and tongue correctly than on dealing with the whole body, and is therefore much more detailed and thorough than I have been here.

- *The Need for Words* by Patsy Rodenburg (Methuen, 1994) is a good exposition of a similar philosophy to this book. It's *much* more advanced, though.